In honor of the life and works of Og Mandino

Og's message of clearer thinking and inspiration changed my life and gives me great will to do the same for others.

LIVING IN THE STORM

Creating Joy and Inspiration When Everything is a Mess

For additional copies of Living in the Storm, please contact:

Living in the Storm
PO Box 4426
Topeka, KS 66604

Twitter: @murnahan
Telephone: 1-866-293-2489 (U.S. and Canada)
Fax: 1-866-293-2489
Skype: murnahan
Website: livinginthestorm.com

First Printing: September 2009

ISBN-13: 978-0-9824978-1-4

Table of Contents

Introduction:

Many moments of joy and inspiration go unnoticed and are overshadowed by the storm that makes up our lives. Recognizing those joys and creating moments of joy and inspiration for others can create a perfect break in the clouds. It may even create the extended break that you have been seeking all along.

Each day of our lives, from the first time we open our eyes and take our first breaths, we receive influences from those around us. We often make our decisions based on their caution, their defeats, and their status quo. Breaking away and creating your own new beam of sunshine between the clouds is not as hard or as frightening once you can feel confident making your own decisions, and creating your own view of what is realistic. Then it is possible to turn the influence around in a positive way.

It may seem easy to trudge through a whole lifetime saying "I could have", "I should have", or "Maybe when the time is right". Unless you already live your wildest dreams, you give yourself reasons that it just did not work out for you. Maybe family got in the way, you did not have enough money, or other short-term issues just stretched out longer than you hoped.

It is time to stop that right now! Let's make a pact. If you will agree to be honest, I will agree to be honest. I am not asking for your honesty to me, but rather to yourself. Level with yourself, and if you can agree that you have let yourself and others down, make this pact with me, and take the care to try a different approach. Deal?

Alright then, today, while the storm is still in full force, you have made a step toward living in the storm, and not just surviving the storm to enjoy life between moments of doubt and confusion.

In the course of this book, I ask that you will draw parallels to your life and use things you know but may be afraid to admit, or may have long forgotten. I will also ask you to perform some tasks that I believe will help you with clearing some of the clouds. In the end, I intend for you to be more influential than influenced, and to share your success with others rather than accept others' defeats as your own.

Just a Little Encouragement

We can take a lot of lessons from kids. In my second day of writing this book, I was reminded how much children can teach us. It is back-to-school time, and a lot of people are highly involved in their children's lives. Parents scramble to shop for backpacks, crayons, pencils, clothes, and then rush to the school for enrollment. Many parents are relieved to see their kids back at school so they can have more peace in their home, and others will miss their little sweethearts. Perhaps many will be torn.

My little four year old girl, Madeline, started school today. She will attend school two hours per day, four days per week, as a third year preschooler. We shuffle a lot around to be sure that Madeline, Simon, and our newborn son, Jack Walden will all be where they should be, and that they are getting all of the best we can provide as parents. One day it is vaccinations for Jack Walden, the next day is "Meet the Teacher Night" at Simon's school, and then a fundraiser for Madeline's school. It all comes at us so fast.

Surely you can cite a similar scramble in your life. Maybe you are the student and you feel this storm from another very stressful point of view. That is definitely not to be overlooked. Students have my great respect, and you will soon know why. Maybe you are new on your job, you just lost a job, you are sick in a hospital, or you love somebody who is. There are so many storms in our lives that there is no way I can recite them all and fit them into a book that you can read within this century.

Whatever your instance, it can get pretty consuming just to keep up with the little things we all deal with each day. While I was dealing with holding down my little corner of the planet this week, I had another of those great realizations of how life really does kind of act like a storm, where everybody gets a different result.

While all of this is back-to-school chaos was going on for me, right in the middle of my storm, my brother rang me on the phone with tragic news that his fifteen year old daughter was sitting in a driveway on the back of a pickup when a drunk driver turned down the wrong street. The driver lost control and hit the pickup at over fifty miles per hour. She was thrown from the truck and into a tree when her pelvis was severely shattered and her intestines punctured. She pulled through a long surgery and she will live, but she is a long wheelchair ride from recovery.

While Maggie is in the hospital, her little thirteen year old brother has found greater than ever ways to dismiss all rules and disappear, as he has done before. He was supposed to be at the library. Yeah, I know that story. I was that kid, once upon a time. My brother struggles with questions of where in the heck his son got a belt displaying marijuana leaves, and why. This is not how he was supposed to be? This is not what a person expects when they do their level best to raise good kids.

The very next day, I received a call that my 92 year old grandmother fell down and broke several ribs. While at the hospital, they gave her Vicodin for the pain, which caused her to be awake all night hallucinating and vomiting. That made the broken ribs even worse. Then she encountered atrial fibrillation and excessive fluid in her lungs. She is now facing a slow and difficult recovery.

How can my struggles possibly compare to that? I seem to have it so good in comparison to so many others in this world, and even in my own family. There are many people struggling and hanging on for life at the end of a gun, or at the end of a disease. Maybe this should boost me up and make me thankful for what I have. Then again, maybe this should depress me and cause me to join in more misery. Maybe the answer is in between the two extremes. Maybe the answer lies in compassion and a realization that the storm is something each of us encounters in a very personal way. We are all in this storm of life, and we can also weather it much better than we often do.

As you read the examples I will share with you in this book, I want you to be reminded that I am not a guy who is writing this to tell you how to live, or how to be. I am simply sharing ideas of how we can each look at things differently. I do not write this from a perspective of anything but genuine life. I am living right there in the storm, where you are. Your experiences in the storm may make mine look like a sunny walk on the beach, or you may wonder how in the world a guy can find optimism and succeed in life with my background. In any case, I want to remind you that we are all people seeking mostly the same outcomes. We desire different things, but what will matter in the end is how we live and how to make happiness thrive, even during the worst of storms.

For my little girl, Madeline, that small bit of encouragement today was so simple. She wanted to go higher on her swing. Instead of only pushing her, I coached her. I recounted her lessons of how to pump her legs, arch her back, develop the rhythm, and swing higher and higher with each swing. It was only a short moment before she was laughing and loving her accomplishment more than ever. She didn't really need a push, because a push was too easy. Just a little encouragement was what made my sweetheart laugh without restraint. She swung higher with encouragement than I may ever dare to push. I hope you will swing higher with encouragement, too, and also never forget how far you may help others to swing if you offer them a similar gift of caring.

The Happy Waiter

I will not claim that a waiter has the happiest job in the world, but I have sure seen some happy waiters. If you consider the work they perform, it should be easy to imagine their joy. You may not see it quite yet, but it seems so obvious to me. The overall function of their job is to give people what they want. This can be said for many professions, but a few things stand out about waiters. They often come into our lives when we are having good times with friends, celebrating, or just meeting to share a meal together. They are there to help us feel good, and extinguish our hunger. They are really a lot more important to us than it may seem at first glimpse.

The happy waiter, the one who really loves what they do, shares their positivity and gives us something to smile about. Perhaps the cynic would say that they are just working hard for a bigger tip, but that is the cynic. Cynicism has no value here.

Can you remember a really happy waiter? I can, and I see them as a great reminder of pride and joy that comes from serving others. In fact, one that comes to mind has not served me in over thirty years. He was a waiter who used to make funny faces at me and my brothers while standing behind our parents. When our parents would look around to see what we were laughing at, he would just shrug and act as if he had no idea what was going on. Maybe you think that I should have little reason to recall this man, but I do, and his name is Mahmoud Nasrazadani. As kids, we thought his name was cool. We never knew somebody with such a unique name, so it stood out, and I still remember his silly antics.

I am not saying that you may remember a waiter from your childhood, but I will say that the cumulative effect of people who treat you nicely and make you smile have much to do with the person you are. Maybe I am one of the few who remember Mahmoud in this way, but how compelling is it to imagine being one of those people that others will remember so many years later?

Of course, this will not be the same for all waiters, and it has much to do with how they see their work. The waiter who will give the best service is the one who truly enjoys creating joy, and you can spot them quickly. They are the kind of people you come back and request when you visit their restaurant. I think we should all try to learn from these people and try to be a happy waiter in our own lives.

The same trait of receiving joy from giving joy is available regardless of your profession or whether you have any job at all. A good lesson I consider is from my 92 year old grandmother who takes time each week to volunteer at "the old folks home". I laugh when I hear her call it that, because many of the residents are much younger than her. She volunteers her time to serve them food and best of all, to make them smile. She is a happy waiter.

The very powerful feelings that come from helping others can be noted as some of the best success stories in your life. Just think for a moment about times that you have done something nice for others, and how it made you feel. There is no doubt that when you do this enough that it can form a truly valuable habit. Other people watch and learn from your actions, and will often follow your lead.

Becoming "The Happy Waiter" can start as simple acts of kindness and consideration of others. If you do it each day, in some way, you should never wonder if somebody received a benefit. The person receiving the greatest benefit is often **you**.

I certainly should mention the downside to being happy by creating happiness for others. There is always the cynical person who will call happy people "fake". Before you decide to be happier by serving joy to others, I must first pose this very important question:

Would you rather receive suspicion of falseness for being happy and spreading joy, or as genuine for being grumpy and cynical?

I would rather be seen as fake for being optimistic than genuine for being a cynic. I know which of these is happier. If you are one of those cynics, you had better stick around and keep reading. You may be really surprised to find how much joy you are missing.

A Second Impression

It is always taught that first impressions are crucial in life. This is mostly accurate, but sometimes it is best to remain open to a second impression. If you can allow negative preconceptions to fade, and take a different second-look, you may stand to gain a lot.

There is an astonishing propensity for immigrants to become successful in America. The same may also be said for immigrants to other countries as well, but since I am in USA, I will use it as an example.

Many immigrants become successful in business, education, family, and overall quality of life in America. Sure, it is not the case for all immigrants, but it is true for a significantly higher percentage of immigrants than natural born citizens. There are a number of obvious reasons for this, and there is a lot of screening in the immigration process to weed out bottom-feeders. There is a high barrier of entry. As any legal immigrant can explain, it is not a simple task to pick up roots and move to another country.

Why are these people successful? One reason could certainly be said that these are people who persist in chasing their dreams. They have set long-term goals and are willing to do whatever it takes to reach them. Once they have committed to the long journey, it becomes impossible in their minds to break down and give up. They know what they want, and they will make it happen. They take lessons from adversity, rather than accepting defeat. They are strong-willed, and ready to face the storm.

Reasons for immigrant success go far beyond the challenges. A perfect setting for success was created by a desire that began long before they ever stepped foot on American soil. They saw a vision of opportunity, happiness, and freedom. They do not only *think* these things exist, but instead, they *know* it. The dream becomes a part of them, and nearly everything they do is aimed toward their goal.

They see something that many people take for granted, and they see it without all of the roadblocks in the way. They have a success-oriented mindset. They look beyond the roadblocks to see the end-result of having the life they want.

It is easy to see this behavior in other relocations as well. A similar attitude of success often occurs when people move to a new city. They have all new surroundings with many new opportunities to make a better life.

I will not tell you to pack up and move to another country, or another city. A new location is not the answer, but rather a new perspective. When you make a commitment to reevaluating your surroundings, it is refreshing. When you start envisioning things with possibility rather than defeat, life feels a whole lot better. When you are willing to commit to a similar level of dedication to your goals, like that of an immigrant, the reasons for failure will diminish every step of the way.

Being Thankful and Apologetic

Saying "Thank you" and "I am sorry" are important, and may not only make a difference for others, but they can change how you view yourself. It is best, even in the most extreme storms that challenge your life, to remember the importance of being thankful for others' kindness and sorry when you are wrong. I often find that the two are related, and that those who are thankful and apologetic are the most caring people. Caring is a good thing. Caring does not only create an outward appreciation of you, but also gives you reminders that can feel really good.

Thank You!

Whether it is as simple as a stranger holding the door for you, or a friend going above and beyond all expectations, a "Thank you" can mean a lot. It is not only a kindness to give it, but it is also a reminder to feel thankful.

Much of my communication with others occurs by way of Internet and telephone. I am a big fan of technology. However, I still find that a good old fashioned hand written thank you holds a much greater value to me. It took more time from the sender, and shows care. When I receive them, it often makes me want to send them a thank you for the thank you, except that would possibly create a really crazy cycle.

I am Sorry

Saying "I am sorry" is a simple way to check your ego and to regain another's confidence in you and make a new start. Avoiding all causes to ever say "I am sorry" is even better, but that does not always work.

An apology is one of the worst horrors that many people may imagine. A public apology is the worst tragedy for some people. A connotation that is taken from the simple words "I am sorry" is that one person is wrong and another is right. I learned somewhere that an apology meant I was wrong, and so I always looked for less self-deprecating terms. If you do not have to lower yourself to apologize, it is best, right? Wrong! This is not always the case. You do not always have to be wrong to apologize, but you are likely to always be right that you do.

Have you ever done something wrong without apology? I have, and until I take the care to make apology, it nags me relentlessly. It is like a dark cloud that looms overhead. I believe that even the little instances can add up and if you neglect them, the extra negativity left behind is simply not worth anything you save. If you have wronged somebody, tell them you are sorry. Give them an opportunity to let go of any frustration they have held toward you. You will often find that you will have done a great service to them and to yourself as well.

Have you ever heard a story of a pet being struck by a car? I use this as an example, because I have seen it many times, both with my pets and those of friends. I have lived in the country where dogs run free. Many of them learn the rules of the road and will look before crossing, but tragically, they do get killed.

Recalling the many dogs and cats I have seen killed or been made aware of from friends' experiences, the most common thing I hear is, "They didn't even stop."

Sure, once the damage is done to the animal, there may not be anything they can do to bring the pet back to health. The damage to the pet is done, but the damage to the person losing a pet has just begun. I know I have thought "Why didn't they just stop to say they are sorry?" I think this is a common feeling, even though it would not make the loss feel a whole lot easier. I think the hardest part is the feeling left behind for the pet lover that "people just don't care".

If you put yourself in the driver's seat, you can rationalize and say that you couldn't do anything to miss the animal, which is normally true. It is not your fault that the animal crossed the road at that wrong time. What do you really have to be sorry for?

Although it is not easy, being the person responsible enough to stop and give a sincere apology for their loss is the right way to be. It shows caring, and it is good for both parties. If you try to apply this to other instances in life, it becomes easy to imagine how apologies can be healing, both for the giver and the recipient. With that in mind, I suggest trying your best to never be the speeding car that just keeps going.

Wins and Losses of Cynicism

You want to win, but sometimes winning is not worth somebody else's defeat. This is especially true if your win is *defined* by their defeat. If you ever find yourself feeling like another person's loss is your gain, it may be a reason to look a little closer at your motivations.

Cynics come in varying levels of intensity, but one thing they have in common is that they do not seem to like it when anybody else has a success. They do not feel good about somebody else's benefit, and I would even call them the anti-soul, because they suck the soul right out of people. I want to show some real life instances of cynicism, but first, I will share a couple of definitions I found for the word cynical.

1. Distrusting or disparaging the motives of others.

2. Bitterly or sneeringly distrustful, contemptuous, or pessimistic.

An argument can be made that some level of cynicism is healthy and that it will keep you out of trouble. There are some really bad people out there in the world with bad motivations and who will hurt you for their own interests. Making the assumption that this is the rule instead of the exception is dangerous, and it can lead to a very bad pattern of destruction.

Living in the Storm

You have surely known a person you could call a "bad sport". Sportsmanship is a positive thing. Striving to do something well can teach some great lessons. Bad sportsmanship occurs when the importance of others losing becomes joyful, instead of the excitement of winning. The feeling some people will carry that they gain from another person's loss is failure-oriented thinking. I see this even more from fans than I do from sports figures. Just walk into a sports bar on game day to see what I mean. You can see many people excited to call somebody a loser for cheering for the losing team.

A large dose of cynicism washed over the world in 2009 as financial giants failed, across the USA and around the world. Wall Street brokers became villains, and distrust was spread far and wide. The distrust was strong enough to cause a domino effect of failures. The fingers were pointing in all directions, and it seems that Wall Street brokers got a huge share of the blame. Did this mean all brokers? The troubling truth is that for an astonishing number of people, it became the fault of all banks, all mortgage companies, and all brokers. The world was caving in, but at least we had people to blame. Cynicism has a strong influence in markets, and this is an example when cynicism hit a high point.

Try to picture for a moment that you are one of the good brokers. You have worked your whole life to do all of the right things, and you are, in reality, far removed from those who caused all of the troubles for others. You never did the things that would eventually crush other people's dreams and take away their sense of security. You really are the good guy. How hard is it to go to work and hear how bad you are? How much does the cynicism of the whole world around you make you want to just stay in bed and pull the blankets over your head … bullet-proof blankets, even? Yes, cynicism has made you a villain, and it will take a long time and a lot of struggle to overcome it. You may always be the bad one, just by association. You may come out stronger and better than ever, but was it really right of others to make assumptions about your integrity?

A lower-level of cynicism can be seen in many lesser things around you. I remember feeling ashamed for many people a number of years ago when I helped some friends organize a garage sale. I watched people attempt to negotiate the price of nice things that they really wanted that were already ridiculously low priced. One example was a pair of shoes that had been worn once and were in perfect condition. They were the right size, and one lady liked them. The shoes were in their original box along with a receipt which showed they had cost about $150 only a year earlier. I recall the lady trying to negotiate the fifty cent price tag on them. I remember others who were not willing to give twenty five cents for items, but would pay a dime. The point that bothers me is not that somebody wants a good bargain. That is why they got up early to beat all the others to the first garage sales.

The problem I see with the instances I mention here is that they are not looking out for themselves nearly as much as they simply do not want somebody else to get what they want. I mean, really, unless they are one of those people who horde everything they can drag into their packrat-like midden, they cannot possibly save enough money to make it worth their time, or the hassle and defeat of the seller.

As a marketing professional for over twenty years, I have had a high level look at cynicism each day. In marketing, it is important to express what the target audience will receive. Looking at a product or service from a consumer's point of view is very important. Realizing how a cynic will see it is also very important. We must often assume, in the beginning, that they are all a bit cynical to some degree.

Many cynical people see a marketing message as an underhanded attempt to take away people's money for something they do not need. Certainly there are instances of this, but there is often a lot of benefit that people can gain. Just consider how you would ever have learned about most of the products or services around you if not for the creation and implementation of a marketing plan. It is how we learn about new things, and can be very helpful. Most people and companies are not out to hurt those they serve. Instead, successful people and companies realize that helping others to get what they want is the best way to get what you want.

You can encounter instances of cynicism in everything from a drive through busy traffic to the person who assumes the worst when you buy them flowers for no apparent reason. Some are more destructive than others, but it is an overall bad feeling to carry. Cynicism breeds cynicism, and it often starts from within, by doubting one's own intentions. Making efforts to let go of your own cynicism, knowing your intentions, and doing the right things for the right reasons are great steps toward eliminating it in yourself and others.

If you focus more on the importance of helping others to get what they want, you stand a much greater chance of getting what you want. Getting this wrong and trying to do it the other way around is popular, but absurd.

Children Singing or a Car Crash

When you turn on the evening news, consider which you are more likely to find; children singing in a school musical or a car crash. You may find both at times, but let's face it, bad news sells. If you count the stories of tragedy and the stories of happiness, it is easy to see which is more popular. Even on a day filled with good news, just consider which stories stand out in your mind the most. This is not a fault of media alone, but rather the fault of an audience who want shock, horror, and to see the worst in humanity. It is a big audience, and they are all around you. Most will not openly admit their negativity, and most do not even admit it to themselves.

Anybody who has spent much time in a car has probably seen the aftermath of a car crash. Fire trucks and ambulance are there, doing their best to help, while cars line the road and slowly pass by the wreckage. Have you ever wondered why people crane their neck when they see a highway traffic accident? Are they looking to see that everybody made it out and will be fine, or are they looking at the destruction? If they see broken bodies and bloody teddy bears will it make them feel better? I believe the answer is that it becomes a part of them. I have seen people die, both on television and in person, and I do not like it, not even a little bit. Finding entertainment in somebody else's' pain and suffering will not make life better.

Living in the Storm

I have asked a question of others many times that gives an illustration of emotional attachment to either misery or joy. I will ask you the same question: If a friend announces that they just got a new puppy, or if they tell you that their dog just died, which one affects you more profoundly? You do not have to answer me, but rather answer for yourself. Maybe you consider the joy over the sadness, but the truth is that sad and upsetting feelings are much easier to spread than joy and inspiration. That is why I believe in the huge importance of expressing the good news. It may not wash away all of the negative, but it is certainly a good start.

I have heard many people say that the best part of watching a race is the crashes. Looking at that from a different perspective as a driver, I see something totally different. A race without a red flag is preferred. When I see the safety workers all dressed in white and the ambulance and fire crews rushing to rescue a driver, I know that it is going to be a sad day for somebody. Sure, there is a lot of safety gear in a race car and all around the race track, and fatalities are more common as a result of a heart attack than a crash. However, none of that gear can fix the upset to a driver who will not finish the race. It may be entertaining to some, but that is because of a detachment.

The same concern of attachment to positivity or negativity occurs in our lives each and every day. It is not always so traumatic as a car crash or the death of a friend's pet. There are a lot of reasons that people will look for tragedy, but they can also be trained to seek the good news. It is a learning process that starts with a decision you make. If you make the decision, and give yourself reminders each day, the cumulative effect can be amazing.

You Go Where Your Eyes Go

One of my great passions in life is the sport of automobile racing. I love going fast, and I have often said that a day at the racetrack it is the most fun a person can have with their clothes on. I love it so much that I became very good at it. That usually happens when you have a great passion for something. My passion has led me to teaching others the joy of driving.

I am a high performance driving instructor for Porsche Club of America, Audi Club North America, BMW Club, and a couple of race tracks. I also volunteer to instruct young drivers in a safety course called Street Survival. A common lesson I teach is that you will go where your eyes go. This is true, whether it is at 170 miles per hour approaching turn one at Road America, or at 15 miles per hour on a wet skidpad. As an instructor sitting in a passenger seat, my safety often relies on watching the driver's eyes and knowing what they are taking in. If my driver is looking in the wrong place, the car will go there. At high speeds with walls and other cars around, you can bet I am very aware of where they are looking.

A race driver's eyes are never focused on the next turn, but rather what lies beyond the turn. Their eyes are always moving. A great driver's proper use of their eyes is one of their most important assets.

Your eyes only have to see something for an instant, and then you look further ahead. Your brain does the work to achieve the desired outcome, based on the information your eyes saw far in advance. The same is true with every other vision in your life.

Like driving a race car, the further you look ahead in your life, the more the amazing subconscious power of your mind will find the correct path to get you there. Training your visions in life and looking in the right places and not staring at the wall at turn one is challenging. It takes a dedicated decision and a faith in your possibilities. It comes with practice. Also like racing, sometimes you have to go slow to be fast. Avoiding the gravel traps that friends and jealous antagonists will place along the side of the track will take skill, courage, and patience.

Motorcycles Don't Have Training Wheels

Anybody who has ever learned to ride a motorcycle should be able to recall the initial nervousness. It is a bit scary to sit there on a gas powered rocket that could send your body to the ground with just one little slip up. You sit there, remembering the gas, the clutch, the brakes, and then you are supposed to use turn signals, too. Oh yes, and look out for other drivers! When the motor starts, you sit there with your clutch hand shaking and a cramp starting to build from being so tensed up. You decide that if you are ever going to do this, you cannot just sit there idle in the parking lot forever. So you give it a little more gas, jerkily release the clutch, and clunk, the motor dies and the motorcycle lurches forward. Yikes! You tense up even more as the front of the motorcycle is shoved downward and it feels like it is going to flop over on the ground. You may have to walk around to shake off the nerves for a bit, but before you know it, you are ready to give this another try. Why? Because you want to ride, and you are just certain it will be a lot of fun once you learn.

I use motorcycles as an example. Perhaps you have never ridden, but certainly you can consider other things that you have learned, and the apprehension, frustration, and joy that came from mastering it.

Living in the Storm

In my case, I have ridden motorcycles from the time I was a young kid. It is something I have a lot of experience with, but I still find that there is something more to learn. There is always more to learn, regardless how much experience you have. We create lazy habits, too, so that means it is sometimes important to relearn and refresh the right ways to do things.

In 2006 I purchased a motorcycle unlike any I had encountered before. It is ten feet long with a 47 degree rake on the front forks. The rear tire is 330 millimeters wide, the 117 cubic inch performance tuned engine pushes out very ample horsepower, and the high performance clutch is harder to pull than many people can muster. This thing is a beast! The first time I sat on it, I was actually shaking before I even started the engine. I was like a new rider, learning all over again. Strangely, it was a great reminder to do things with more care to details. It was like taking my experience to a new level.

Consider the things that can take you to a new level, and improve your skills. For me, this motorcycle is a good example. If you give a moment to think about what you have mastered, it is time to think about how you can refresh yourself on the basics, and then take on a new level of mastery. When you stop getting better, sometimes the result is that you become lazy and eventually get sloppy.

Altruism Demystified

I have lived much of my adult life seeking validation. I do not mean validation with the negative connotation you would feel about the person needing a pat on the back for every good deed. I mean the kind of validation that makes one feel good about living life well, and developing good relationships with good people.

I think most of us need, or certainly benefit from, those little moments when somebody reminds us of our goodness ... or better yet, our greatness! Think for just a moment about something that really validated you and made you feel amazing. I find it in things my wife or children say, or in a kind book review from a complete stranger who read my work. These are often the moments which carry us high on a cloud all day, and give us much inspiration to smile upon others. All of the sudden it is easier to give those good feelings to a friend. It becomes contagious when you pass along good feelings to others.

You surely know the type of person who creates this snowball effect. They are those people that make you feel good just to be around them. Many times, you may not even pinpoint why, but these are the people who make you feel better just to know them. Should there really be a mystery to this? They bring you up and make you feel better about yourself. They are the ones reminding you how you want to be … they are the people you admire in the kindest way. This should be a good time to consider all of the times they were kind to you, and make a list of people you would like to reward with the kindness you may be holding back or just forgot to give.

When friends beat you to the punch with a kind word or kind deed, it can almost seem like you may not be as genuine if you immediately try to give back. In some busy lives, it may even seem like if you do not return kindness immediately, it may be forgotten. It almost looks like a reminder when somebody is nice to you and, all of the sudden; it is your prompt to do something nice back. You do not really ever want to feel that way, do you?

Wouldn't it be great if you never needed a prompt to be kind to a friend or complete stranger? The good news is that kindness can be habit forming. For some people it becomes so much a part of their life that you almost wonder how you can ever thank them enough. I think that most of us have people who feel this way about us, but can you imagine the circle of kindness and joy you can produce if you become one of those people like the ones you smile about every time you think of them?

The reward of being this person I have described is that as much as it seems they are always so giving and caring, they receive the greater benefit. Let's take a closer look at this: Even the greatest of givers have something to gain. You can call it pure and unselfish altruism, but there will always be something received in return. You may cite Mother Theresa, Gandhi, or your dear grandmother. Yes, these are kind souls and have done many things that may seem very self-sacrificing. Whether they know it on a conscious level or not, people do nice things for others because it feels good. For some people it is simply a reflex, and for others it may take a little more work. You may call it unselfish, but if it did not feel good to them, and if it did not feel right, they would not do the things they do.

So there you have it. Altruism is demystified and the truth is that the reward is just not as it may be expected. I hope you will take some time, right now, to think about how even a small act of kindness can change people's lives. Especially yours! When you are kind to others, it can build a reflex. It can become natural to spread a kind word. When that happens, the good feelings you have about yourself can be shocking!

Validation Earned vs. Validation Demanded

Some people will beg for the kind of validation described here. Maybe they had a lot of validation from a friend, family member, lover, or just received it at every turn in their life. When that goes away, it is easy to become insecure and confuse the order of reward. Rewards come with a reason, and insecurity often prompts people to demand the reward before it is due. This is very easy to see in children as they learn to seek rewards early in life. Many people have a hard time realizing the correct order of rewards. In fact, I think it is something that everybody battles from time to time.

I want to share a story. Yes, I like to tell descriptive stories of how I learned things. I hope that you may find parallels to your storm in some way, and relate it to something that makes sense in your life. Be kind and hear me out.

When I was very young, all eyes were on me. I was the last of eight sons, and a spotlight shined at my every footstep. Of course, with that spotlight, there was also some resentment and torment from the competition. Over all, I guess it was pretty easy to receive validation. As I grew into grade school, the attention got a little tougher. I had to find new ways to get my due attention, and I would keep my star status, whatever it took. Yes, I spent a lot of time in the principal's office, and my parents attended a lot of talks with the teachers.

When I was ten, my father died in a car wreck. Attention would never be the same. It would have to be forced. Oh yes, I became the kid who would do all kinds of bad stuff for attention. I always remember being the kid they talked about as needing much attention. In fact, I took it way overboard as a teenager. I let my mother down. In fact, I did nearly everything a kid could do that would cause shame for a parent. Without getting into great detail just yet, I will say that I probably would not have made it to age sixteen in many households.

As I grew up a bit, I would remember periods when I had earned the attention and validation I needed. I remembered times like when I would wake up very early every morning of fifth and sixth grade, before my brothers, and make breakfast for my mother. I would bring perfectly buttered strawberry toaster pastries and a cup of my best gourmet coffee and serve it in bed just before her alarm would go off. It was my routine, and the one time of day that we could talk about stuff. I was attached to her and I would do anything to be good to her. We really connected after my father's death during the summer before fifth grade. I needed her, and she needed me.

It gave me the feeling that I could do something well, and I could do it right. It was my little bit of altruism in life, but if you think for a moment that it did not mean the world to me, guess again. I still think of those days, and I remember how good it felt to me that I was being her sweet little man. She must have felt a lot about me the way I do with my kids.

Life eventually got in the way of this routine. She got busy, I got busy, and so I needed to seek attention elsewhere. I needed attention that nobody had time for anymore. I caused trouble at school, I caused trouble at home, and I was just generally trouble. I re-learned a bad lesson that I could demand attention, instead of earning it. Only, in this case, as perhaps with many people, I had not made the distinction between positive attention and negative attention. It was a whole lot of the mentality we see around our lives all the time. It is as if to say "What? You don't hear me? Oh, you WILL hear me!"

I grew up with some high-level self-destruction, but I eventually found those memories of positive reinforcement and earning attention instead of demanding it. That will happen for each of us on our own individual terms, and only when we are ready. Once it hit me, I think it opened a lot of old wounds. I think I was finally shaken with enough shame and disappointment in myself that I spent a lot of time trying to make up for those bad decisions. For me, making up for hardships that I caused my family became a centerpiece. It is still a huge factor in my life, but I can truly say that I regained a lot of their respect, and made up for a lot of their resentment. This happened only after I came around to realize the hugely important difference between validation that is earned and validation that is demanded.

Age and Wisdom: A Time Travel

When we are young, we think we know what is best for us. When we are older, we think we know what is best for others, but often give up on ourselves. Whether you are a teen with a dumb parent or a senior who still feels 25, it is time to take inventory, and discover other points of view.

There is a constant storm of ages that blows wildly and throws us into generation gaps and misconceptions about age and wisdom. I was curious about the topic, so I asked somebody older. I guess it just seemed more reliable than asking somebody younger. After all, "I already did that" is the simple attitude to assume. Wow, isn't that an interesting? I already nearly sabotaged the whole concept of bridging a gap and providing varying points of view. I almost relied on a common misconception that age and wisdom are perfectly aligned. I assumed that an older person may have more to share on the topics of age and wisdom than a young person. That sounds like something an old guy would do. How old am I anyway? How old are you? Let us take a little journey through the ages. We can call it a time travel.

We have surely all seen the woman who dresses like her teenage daughter hoping to appear younger. That lady has become an icon of modern society. If you ever saw the movie "American Pie", you may note that Stiffler's mom is a great example of an age, wisdom, and maturity conflict. There are so many conflicts that people have with their age, and related perceptions, that it is hard to count them all. This dilemma has spawned huge industries. Yet, smoking and drinking to act older while young; and surgeries, clothing, diets, exercise, and other methods of age alteration later in life still leave remnants and confusing misconceptions of age in their path.

I remember being excited to get older so that I could finally show my parents how it is really done. Their rules would never exist in my life. I would never make my kids follow rules. Those rules were stupid! After all, how could they possibly know anything about my life?

When I was twelve years old, I was pretty smart as a Boy Scout. I was a Den Leader and teaching the Cub Scouts some necessary skills. I must have known it all. I knew a whole lot of really neat stuff. I knew how to start a fire, pitch a tent, sleep under the stars, and I could teach others to survive in the wild. I was pretty much ready for life. Bring on the wilderness. I am prepared!

As I realized that girls were more than only a *little* interesting, I found that roller skating and cool clothes were up there alongside the importance of making fire and surviving the wild. That was close to the time that my mother lost her head. Like so many other parents, my mother is a survivor of an acute mental retardation that tragically hits parents during the period when their kids are between puberty and parenthood. By the time I was thirteen, it was amazing that she could still get a spoon to her own mouth, much less drive a car. I mean, for several years there, she was as dumb as a marshmallow on a turkey sandwich. I really worried for her. She sounded like a drunken dictator as she would tell me what to do. Nothing came out of her mouth but a bunch of garbled syllables that sounded like a foreign language to me.

Skipping ahead, I remember my mother looking out for me and consoling me after a really hard breakup. Yes, she was still there, telling me what to do. However, her dictatorship was broken, and her scrambled code was getting a little clearer. She helped me through another hard time as she reminded me that not all motivations mix well with love.

I was kind of a show-off in my twenties. I owned several businesses and had all kinds of fun to offer for "Ms. *Right*". Unfortunately, I spent a lot of time with "Ms. *Right Now*". One case was a woman I spent a number of years with. I still respect her for the time we shared, and I credit her with a lot of lessons in how to be a better man, and also how to judge character. Perhaps most importantly, I learned lessons relating to both wisdom and maturity.

While one of my companies was becoming needy of my time and money, which is to be expected by any entrepreneur, my sweetheart was feeling a bit wary of our relationship. Of course, I saw it as coincidental, or that I was probably just working too hard with a lot of irons in the fire. Maybe I was not as giving or easy to enjoy while I was under stress and working hard. Maybe it was just chance that it was the same week I had cut her allowance down to brace for future goals.

My mother said something that I will never shake, and she said it just like this: "Mark, she loves you, and that is easy to see. But I also want to remind you that she loves your money." So, I guess Chops shared some good insight in this case. I call my mother "Chops", because sometimes I just want to go kiss her on the chops, and other times I just beg her to stop busting my chops.

Skip ahead a bit more, after the hard breakup, I went back to my former standard of dating more mature women. Fine, I said mature, but I really meant *much older*. I always saw a big interest in older ladies. The truth is that I really had a hard time relating to people my age back then. After all, I left school years earlier than those my own age, I was raised by a father who was their grandparents' age, and I had brothers older than my mother. Somehow, I just related to ladies 20-some years older than me. Some people would call these ladies a "Cougar", which is commonly defined as a woman over 35 who seeks much younger men. Chops usually called them something else. Yes, *something* else.

This time, Chops' wisdom hit me between the eyes as something I already knew. I wanted children one day. My girlfriends already had grandchildren, which is purportedly awesome. However, that was ultimately a big skip ahead for me. I would have missed a lot if Chops' wisdom had not been there by my side. I probably would have become a home wrecker and run off with one of my girlfriends' daughters if left to my own reasoning.

When I was thirty, I met my oldest son at his birth. To give it to you in generational terms, he was really "kick ass". I was "Daddy" now, and surely I would have the opportunity to set all new standards. I would know more than my parents. I would demolish all of those rules they had when I was a kid … right? Fine, you called my bluff. We packed him in the car and we were ready to head home. The first thing I said to my wife was "OK, I guess we are all ready to go. So what's next?" We laughed a little, nervously. I said to Peggy, "Did we get an owners' manual?" Oh, come on, if you are a parent, you can surely remember the terror of the first moment you were set loose on the world with a person to raise. You saw how it was done all through your life. You surely had parents, and they must have taught you all of the wrong stuff to do, right? As long as you do nothing at all the same as your parents did, that should work.

I can laugh about this so much now, but the funniest thing is that my first reaction was "Mommy! I need help!" Chops had brainwaves after all this time. It was a miracle!

Confusion and frustration of age hit me pretty hard as a young businessman. I was always a bit too anxious to get older. I knew that age would bring more credibility, and it was a long hard wait. I could not even take a client out for a drink for my first several years in business. I just wanted to spring forward to my forties, when people would take me more seriously in business. Others shudder at the thought of turning forty, and I have even heard people expressing stress at turning twenty-five.

Many people take age very seriously. It can cause frustration that life just is not what they wanted by whatever age marker they set. Age can cause a rift in a marriage due to insecurities. Many people question, "How can my spouse still find me attractive at this age?" Some can take a joke pretty well on the surface, but feel something else deep down. When my wife turned 35, I joked that based on her real age and my mental age she can be my "Cougar" and I can be her prey. She is actually younger than me, so I hope she gets the joke.

When I asked for Chops' view of age, she told me that aging is hard. She said that she still feels young and thinks young, but it hurts for people to look at her as so much older than she feels. I told her that when my wife, Peggy and I talk about age, it feels like we are at least ten years younger. We note that when we see others our age, we often see them as much older than us. Sometimes we are shocked by meeting people much younger and just assuming they are older than we are. Chops said that many older people, including her, feel exactly the same way. She told me this with some qualification. She lives in a retirement community since my stepfather's stroke has made it much harder for him to get around. She talks to the retirees. She also talks on the subject with her mother who at 92 years old has never seen herself as old.

If it is true for you that you still feel much younger than your body tells you, you are not alone. Minds seem to age much slower than bodies. It can cause a huge internal conflict if you let it. Something we should all remember is that we are all exactly the age set by a calendar. You are exactly the age you are supposed to be.

Are you too old? Are you too young? The calendar dictates a number, but you are in charge of what that number means to you. You are never too young to teach nor too old to learn. You have much value to offer others, whatever your age. So, when you question the best age to be, I hope your answer is the age you are *right now*.

Weight: A Heavy Subject

The subject of weight is a very sensitive point for a lot of people. In fact, it is the worst of all storms in many people's life. When it is your body, it is not something you can put on a shelf and deny. That weight is everywhere you go, which makes it a very hard issue to endure. The physical health concerns of obesity are daunting, and the mental health concerns are often even worse.

For the vast majority of people concerned by their weight, there is good news. You are not as fat as you think. Certainly, this is not always the case, but I will get to that. First, let us consider a lifetime of illusions that are imposed upon us about weight.

I remember a contraption in our home when I was a kid. It was taller than me, and looked very heavy duty. It was designed for a person to stand on its platform with a belt around the waist to let it shake the fat away. This medieval contraption I have described is one of countless fads in a multibillion dollar industry. It is a very driven industry that tells us all what looks good, and how we should be. I think that machine was once my mother's best hope of never getting up to 130 pounds. That did not work out for her. She should get her money back. My mother is not huge by any means, although she does have a thyroid disorder that requires constant medication. Sure, she has reason for concern, but I remember her thinking she was fat in her thirties when she was actually a rail.

Concerns of weight can begin very young, and often start at home. Has your mother ever blamed you for her excess weight? Go ahead, raise your hand, I am. There goes my wife's hand waving high. Maybe it is not as common as I think, but I have heard this from countless mothers, "I was not fat until I had kids." The problem with this is twofold. First, there is the question of whether those kids were worth the extra hips. The bigger concern is in passing along feelings of negativity for being too heavy. This reinforces bad feelings for mother and instills ideas about weight for the child.

Body image is yet another example of how we take influence from everybody around us. It often affects us far more than we can consciously define. I remember hearing how little I was as a kid and looking around at all the other huskier kids on the playground. I have never been a very large man, and I have spent much of my life concerned about being too thin. It seems that nobody has much compassion for that. The truth from a small person is that it can hurt just as much. I hated feeling like a skinny little guy, but I eventually accepted that I was just an economy-sized person. Others were built to be big. One of my closest friends jokes that he weighed more in eighth grade than I do today. He is just two inches taller than me, but he would look like a scarecrow if he weighed within eighty pounds of my weight. Becoming comfortable with other areas of life can make the matter of body image feel much better. I may be small, and you may be big, but maybe we are just right after all.

Obesity and Morbid Obesity

Feeling comfortable with yourself is important, but feeling comfortable with an unhealthy body is not. If you have a body mass index of thirty, you are obese. If your body mass index is forty or greater, you are morbidly obese. These are not insulting terms meant to hurt you, but rather clinical statements of fact.

I want the best for you, and I want you to make good choices. I want you to make better choices today than you did yesterday. The same rules of focusing on the positives in your life hold true, and if you are obese, that counts double for you. It is clearly time to make better decisions and create a new cause for joy in your life.

Sure, there are some people who say they are proud to be obese, but vanity is claimed in many unexpected forms. The irrefutable fact is that obesity is extremely unhealthy and can cause many other problems that destroy quality of life. Something important to note is that the biggest contributing factor is behavior. If you eat too much, you will get bigger. If you do not exercise, you will remain that way.

Very few people will look at their 64 inch waistline and say, "Yep, that's my fault … I screwed it up." Like any challenge, there are countless excuses to fail. There are at least as many excuses for obesity as there are obese people. There are also many stories of others with a much tougher battle that succeeded once they made a committed decision. I recall watching a documentary on the heaviest man on earth that showed how he exercised in bed. It looked like all of that weight was going to rip his legs off as he struggled along. If you think it cannot be done, it cannot, but if you think it can be done, it can.

Failing at weight control is a matter of life or death to many people, and yet they choose death. The excuses win over all of the reasons to change. The good news for you is that you have made a decision to look at life differently, and to live in the storm rather than just wait for it to blow over. You understand that it takes a decision, and that it will take work. I do not need to point out all of the medical reasons to make this decision. You have heard about diabetes, heart disease, and many other disorders related to obesity. You know the risks, and you know the rewards. It will take self-control and it will take exercise. It will not be simple, but could there be a better time to start? You remember that honesty pact we made, right? The next time you look at that extra slice of pizza or doughnut, force yourself to be honest.

You Want Money First?

Since I recognize that economic stress is one of the first reasons a lot of people may pick up this book and read it, let us examine this. Yes, economy is on the mind of much of the world's population today ... every day. Maybe personal financial struggle is on your mind right now. This is likely just as it was in your best of times, and as it will be until you put it back into perspective as the after-effect that it truly is in your life.

I do not want you to feel let down when I tell you that your own personal finance actually comes last in the improvements of living in the storm. Just to make it feel better, I will tell you that if you get all of the other pieces just right, economy will not fail you. Money is a side-effect of doing things right, thinking well, and making good decisions even while in the most forceful storms of life.

You can assume that economic factors are totally out of your control. When you hear a lot of negativity about the global economy and that people all around you are suffering, it is easy to believe that the ship is sinking. So, you grab a chunk of wood and try to stay afloat. Joining the crowd in misery is not the right answer. Did you ever hear of cult leader Jim Jones? He got people to join in his misery and look what happened. I beg you; just don't drink the Kool Aid!

I have been wealthy and I have been "peas and pancakes poor", so I will share an observation I have made: It is easy to make bad decisions, and easy to create your choice of joy or misery, with or without money. Money can certainly make some things easier, but when the concept is confused, it can also cause a huge downfall.

I said "peas and pancakes poor", and that was not just some clever bit of wit or an exaggeration. That is a term I use for a very true point in my life when I literally had nothing in the cupboard but some canned peas and powdered pancake mix. I also had a pregnant wife, a growing company to run, and some decisions to make that would either improve my life or crush it. That is a really hard time to make long-term decisions, because survival is in the balance. Today I feel really good about the decisions I made, but let me tell you that it was very hard. I am proud of the things I did, and the strength I gained by looking ahead of life's storm and toward a brighter time in the future.

As much as it may seem that those days were some of my worst, looking back, they are some days that really showed me my strength and perseverance. Even if your storm is raging right now, you must have faith in the lessons you will gain. Maybe you lost your job, you are worried that your electricity will be shut off, or your home is in foreclosure, but there is strangely a positive side. Even now, you can surely look back to a worse time in life when you came out stronger following the adversity. If this really is the very worst of times that you can recall, use this lesson of your strength as you move forward, and keep these times near your heart. These moments of struggle are an important point of comparison between the good and bad times. If you never had hardship you may never recognize the joy in your life.

It amazes me today how much openness I find when the subject of financial hardship comes up. It seems to me that people are more willing to open up and be accepting of the challenges they face. Maybe it is just a bit along the lines of the old saying "Misery loves company", but I think it is more than that. As so much of our world has been challenged all at once, it seems that a lot of people stopped being so ashamed to admit their hardship. It may also be because it just got a whole lot harder to hide it. Whatever the case, I do not think of these people as despicable or like poison. I do not believe you do, either. Just because of a financial hardship, it would seem pretty cold and uncaring to look down at somebody. There are some pretty bad poor people, and some pretty bad wealthy people. Why make assumptions based on their finance? Finances can change a lot faster than ethics.

Think about this really hard. If you would not look down at somebody for not having money, why would you be ashamed of yourself for the same thing? That seems counterproductive to me, but I see it all the time. It seems that if you are poor, everybody loves you, but you hate yourself. That just does not seem right to me in the slightest way. It torments me to see people so wrapped up in an image of having money, or not having money. I remember feeling really proud of myself at times that I was as broke as it gets.

It is also important to question why so many people look at those who do have money with anger or resentment. So which do you want to be? If you do not look at people without money in a negative light, why would you look at somebody with money in a negative light? If you look at somebody with a lot of money and you dislike them for that, wouldn't it be hypocritical of you to ever try to live outside of poverty?

Here is a little story of my life in 2006 that may make you mad at me, because I had a lot of money. In fact, if you are *that* type who will look at somebody in a nice car or a nice home and resent them, I want your full attention here. Get mad at me, hate me, and find all the reasons possible that you want to never be like that. I will be sure to share enough that, if you are one of those who make assumptions based on people with or without money, to really make you think I am an ass. In the end, you may find that if you took this as a reason to dislike me, you were probably totally wrong for that as well. You should know that just because somebody has more money that it is not the reason you have less.

In late 2005, I decided that our newly built home was everything we could ever want it to be, and much more. We made it really spectacular … it is top-notch. So, I thought maybe I would buy myself a nice car. I wanted something safe for the family, and I wanted something unique. I called a friend and said "I want to buy a red Hummer H2 with every option". A couple days later, I went to pick up my new monster truck, and it was pretty awesome. It was a fun truck to drive, even though a lot of people would give me the finger or intentionally cut me off in traffic. I guess I was unwittingly the rich, arrogant jerk in the big red Hummer. No, I was not the guy who made huge sacrifices and worked tirelessly for his dreams. I was the bad guy. Heck, I did not intend it to be that way, but I cannot control others' hate.

Peggy warmed up to driving the behemoth. She liked it, too, but she had been thinking of downsizing to a sedan. She had been driving a Dodge Durango, which is a nice sized SUV, but she thought a BMW sedan would be nice. The make or model was no big deal to her. She just wanted to get where she wanted to go, and have a safe car.

About a few weeks later, a friend called me on the phone and asked if I wanted to go to an auto auction with him. I said "Sure, but please remind me that I am not going to buy anything." We went to a huge auction where a car lover could easily get carried away. I passed by many cars and thought "Hmm, Peggy would like that." I kept my cool, and thought I would come out with all of my money. No, that would not happen on this day. I saw a really beautiful Jaguar that matched all of the other red cars and motorcycles in the garage, and although it was used, it only had about 7,500 miles on the odometer and it smelled and looked like it just came off the showroom. The gavel banged, and I called Peggy. Her first words were, "OK, what did you buy?" I asked her to call our insurance guy to get it insured so I could bring it home to her. She drove it a few times, but one day she said "It is a beautiful car, but after driving the Hummer, it feels strange. It is definitely not a Hummer." Noted!

A month later, we took a little family trip to Houston, Texas, where we love to spend time in the museums and the aquariums. One day, while we were driving to dinner, I drove by a Hummer dealership and I said to Peggy, "Do you mind if I run in there really quick to see about a high-flow air filter?" I wanted the Hummer to have a little more power, since we were spending a lot of time on busy Texas highways. She said, "Yes, I mind. We have reservations, and we need to go." I rephrased it and said, "I am going to run into this Hummer dealership really quick … it will just take a moment."

Well, they did not have what I wanted, but they did have a nice shiny new Hummer H2 that they wanted to make me a really great deal on. We drove across the huge lot to go and take a peek. Suddenly, we had twin Hummers. She liked the "old one", so the new one would be my car.

A month later, it was time for a birthday. Peggy was born on the same day of Pablo Picasso's death. Not only was this a coincidence, Peggy is also an accomplished artist. Yes, you guessed it; I bought her a Picasso for her birthday. Unfortunately, it had not returned from the shop where I had them framing it in a very special museum quality frame to match our home's décor. So, I had to go get something to put a bow on. I called around and I found a really cool gift. A brand new shiny black Corvette should do the trick, and I would give her the Picasso after we returned from our big spending trip to Las Vegas for her birthday.

A month later, we were remembering the new Cadillac Escalade we saw at the dealer when we were buying the second Hummer. I told my dealer friend where I buy my Corvettes that we may be interested in one of those. He had one with every single option, and he said it was ordered by a man who refused to pick it up when he realized how much the new model caused his two year old Escalade to depreciate. Plus, the $68,889 price tag kind of freaked him out. So that day we drove over and bought her a new Escalade.

Apparently the Picasso, the Corvette, the Escalade, and the huge spending spree in Las Vegas impressed her. It was not long before we were at a huge motorcycle rally and show. We saw a huge display of Roger Bourget motorcycles, and our jaws dropped. I only had two bikes in the garage, and they were cool and all, but these were truly rolling works of art. She picked one out for me and said, "I think you should have this one, Mark." I kind of chuckled and said, yeah, if I want to spend more on a motorcycle than I did for my first two homes, combined. She made her case, and talked about how good I have been as a husband and father, and that she would really like me to have something special just for me. Well, I didn't have a checkbook with me, but fortunately I had credit cards. We took it home that day.

When we got home, I ordered another Corvette to replace the one that almost had 1000 miles on it by that time. Four months to the day after I bought the Corvette, I traded it in on one that had the right options.

Oh the stories go on. I have had a lot of fun spending money. My wife likes concerts, and prefers to be right at the stage. Since concerts are an easy time to have a couple drinks, of course, you need a limousine. The trouble is that if you have a whole limousine, it is more fun to fill some of those many seats, so you need to bring a bunch of friends along. But wouldn't it be rude to invite them and expect them to pay for tickets and drinks? Of course that would be rude, who would do that? I really wouldn't want to say how much money we threw at concerts.

Spending money on concerts was always fine with me though, because I race cars. Racing a couple of brand new Corvettes is a really easy way to spend $5000-10,000 per weekend just on wear and tear. In fact, it is one of the easiest ways to blow a couple hundred thousand bucks per year without any expectation of earning any of it back.

So you can make a lot of assumptions about this, right? I told you that I would make you think I am an ass. That was intentional. Surely, there is something wrong with somebody spending that much money. It must be a really sick person to have a bunch of money, and to buy things like that. Well, not really. The most fun spending is to load up a couple of Hummers with toys for a local toy drive, and then write them big checks to be sure that no child has to go without a toy at Christmas. It is fun to go to a March of Dimes motorcycle rally and donate generously. It is fun to give scholarships to hard working students. It is fun to make anonymous donations. It is fun to know that you can give more to others than you ever had before ... and without a need to be recognized. That is what feels good! Money for the sake of money alone is not what heals, and is not what is important. Have faith, my friend, and just trust me on this.

The most important moments in my life come from having lunch at my son's school, or picking him up each day at school and watching our preschool daughter give him a big hug and say "I love you Simon", and then both of them turning to our little baby Jack Walden and giving him a kiss on the cheek. That is the stuff that matters the most, and that is what we live for. Not only do these moments bring us huge pride today, it encourages us because we know that as they grow they will understand and adopt the same values of caring for others. That legacy matters more than any amount of money.

Misconceptions about money, whether in good times or bad, have little to do with the heart of the person. Peace and joy are side-effects of making good decisions, and cannot be demanded, with any amount of money.

Perhaps the strangest part of all this is that for as much as we have always given of ourselves, and our money, we have sometimes felt really awkward for having fine things. We gained an understanding that people often look down upon the wealthy, more than they look down upon the poor. So tell me, how does either one make sense unless you factor in jealousy and other equally miserable negative feelings?

Try looking at money as a tool. Like any other tool, money can have good or bad uses. A hammer can build a home, or it can take a life. How you choose to use it is more important than the device.

When money takes too important a role in families, the tragedy it can cause often affects more lives than the selfish or misinformed ones concerned about the money.

It often shatters the harmony in my family life when we hear of friends getting divorced. I will never feel really settled about dividing families for selfish reasons or troubles that could be avoided. It bothers me greatly how often the reason people refuse to work together relates to their concerns of money, or that money is where they place the blame. Divorce is too often on the tail of somebody losing a job, or some other economic distress. When my wife hears the news of another family destroyed by divorce, it is always met with tears and sorrow, and with a wonder of whether we could have done something to help if we had known soon enough. No, neither of us are practicing psychologists, and we certainly have no delusions about marriage. We just know a whole lot about what it takes to not only sustain a marriage, but how to make it thrive, even in the worst of storms.

It is easy to blame money for many evil things. It causes fights between couples, it causes battles between companies, and it causes wars between nations … right? I believe otherwise. Money, in itself, does not do these things. An unrealistic view of money and an unreasonable desire for more money is what causes these troubles. When you want more power in your life, I would suggest love **over** money. With caring and compassion, you can build a lot of power … the good kind of power. Love for mankind can build the type of power that, in the long run, will provide you with a whole lot more money.

It may sound really silly, but it seems that I see a lot more people who are bad with money than I see bad people with money. Some people just get lucky, but it is very common that those who have earned a lot of money have also contributed to a lot of other people's hopes and dreams. Whether this means they helped more people to have a job, or many other possibilities, the ones who earned their money usually have an interesting story to tell. It usually does not come easily. They have often worked very hard and made a lot of difficult decisions along the way.

Kids are Resilient

You have likely witnessed or at least heard somebody say that kids are resilient. Do you ever question why? Let us consider this for a moment.

All summer long, my children excitedly waited for the sun to rise so they could put on their swimsuits, swim goggles, be slathered with sunscreen, and given the approval that it is time to swim. My kids love playing in the pool, just as I did when I was young.

In my hometown, it is that time of year when the seasons are changing and kids make a transition. Only yesterday, as my wife was closing down our swimming pool, my daughter was riding her tricycle around, as happy as ever. She did not express even a moment of sadness about the pool being closed. This may not seem extreme, but for something that means so much to her, this was a big transition. While Mommy was closing down the pool, Madeline's focus had already shifted to the excitement of decorating our home for Halloween. Negativity was absent from her mind, and she only looked forward.

A more extreme example of kids' resilience is found in the death of a pet. We encountered the death of two pets this year. The first was BeeBah, the family fish. He was a good fish, and the kids loved him. A few months later, our dear old kitty, Alex, passed away after a long bout with age. She was a very old kitty. She slowed down like a wind-up toy running out of spring tension and finally came to rest after about fifteen good years of life.

In both cases of death in our family, there were brief somber moments of reflection, but there was an overall affirmation of life rather than disappointment of death. Some people will maintain this positivity, but it is clearly more present in children.

If you begin to question how that positivity of children is so strong, you may find that the answers lie both in things they have not learned, and also in what they have learned. They don't have all of the bad lessons of negativity yet. They are always looking forward, and do not have negativity to reflect back upon. They also have encouragement and support from others at levels that often fade with time.

When a child attempts a new task, whether it is walking, writing their name, or riding a bicycle, they will normally stumble a few times before they get it right. In the case of riding a bicycle, they often have physical proof of their failure. Why don't they just give up?

Consider the very important factors that influence a child's persistence. First, consider that they have not yet learned that it cannot be done. They do not have concrete proof of the impossible. Even if a kid is told that they will never be able to ride a bicycle, they will not let go of their hopes easily. They see other kids doing it, so it must be possible. They seek ways to adapt that possibility to their own life. They may eventually give up, like an adult will, but they have positivity in great supply. Where do they get all of that positivity? It is important to realize the power of encouragement that a child often receives. They have a cheering section. They receive much support from a parent, sibling, or friend who encourages them to keep trying until they get it right. The encouragement is reinforced with pride in small achievements and strong hopes of mastering the task.

When negative lessons of failure come into our lives, as they often will, and we no longer have the high level of encouragement from others, we let go of hope much sooner. Reevaluating failures and reassembling our cheering section as adults can be challenging, but can also create amazing results. Reevaluating your failures based on your own experiences, rather than the experiences of others, can give you a different outlook. Creating the cheering section can be a lot easier than you may expect.

Negativity Observed: Birth to Death

When a baby is born, it is an amazing thing. The innocence is so obvious. I cannot imagine that anybody could ever fault a baby for having any nefarious intentions. Although they can sometimes seem demanding, surely nobody could fault their character. They really do not want a lot of things. They want food, they want shelter, and they want the very basics of security. The first thing we give them, before anything else, is love.

A tragic outcome of giving love can come with a side-effect of negativity that is taken so deeply that it becomes a big part of that baby's life. The protection of love is never intentionally hurtful, but yet, it may hold that baby back from many proud moments of achieving their dreams.

Perhaps you will not be surprised to find that you are that baby. Others have cautioned you all your life and your failures have created that same caution within you. Maybe you failed at things and it seems like kindness to pass along your wisdom to those you love. A greater kindness may be to realize that, although it may have broken your spirit, another person with another approach may be able to succeed where you failed. Taking that hope away from them may not be so kind after all. Maybe somebody was not so kind to you, too. It is time to analyze it and start to make amends.

You've Been So Wrong

Maybe you will say "that sounds kind of insulting, Mark", and I understand. I want to assure you that I mean this in the kindest possible way. I do not just mean you, I mean all of us. Each and every one of us has been guilty of the unkindness I am about to describe.

Remember that honesty pact we shared in the introduction of this book? Now is when I need you to be as honest as you can be. You have been wrong. Not only have you neglected much of your own passion, you have snuffed out many dreams of those you care about, too. I am not saying that you are mean, or that you must be punished. After all, you care about these people, and you want to share your words of caution and restraint. You want what is best for them.

Realizing, with all "maybes" aside, that you have stolen, cheated, and brutally destroyed somebody's dream is a step in the right direction. Once you realize this fact, it can also be a lot easier to recognize how cynical and negative you have become, in the name of realism and protection.

It is kind of a hard pill to swallow, isn't it? When you start looking inward at the cause, it can be an even darker place. I do not mean that you would ever intentionally hurt those around you, or that you have a single angry bone in your body. What is really dark lurks in the shadows of how you got that way in the first place. It came from somebody who cares about you enough to share their same concern that you give those around you. Although it is often not meant to be anything but kind, our friends, family, and everybody else surrounding our lives teach us to be this way.

Is there a way to change it? That is almost like asking if there is a way to break a cycle of child abuse, drug use, or breaking away from a ghetto. We become cast in the society we come from, and breaking that cast is often seen as something that is only for the few fortunate ones. Who are these fortunate people?

You may call me one of the fortunate ones, but I am here to tell you that good fortune has little to do with it. That assumption is as cynical as it gets because it demeans the value of work. Getting what you want from life and breaking the mold takes work. It takes dedication, strength, disappointment, and often a whole lot of tears. However, before any of these things, it takes a decision!

Deciding to break old habits that have been bestowed upon you by the good intentions of somebody you care about and respect can almost feel like you are thumbing your nose at their love. After all, you are going to prove them wrong … right? No, this is not the case. Instead, you are going to prove why you are worth their consideration and why you are worth their concern. For the ones who gave you negativity out of jealousy, yes, it may feel kind of good to prove them wrong. For the largest part, you will make people proud, and make people even more endeared to you. Perhaps the biggest fright is that it will filter out the differences between those with good intentions and those hoping to hold you back for selfish reasons.

Tough Decisions

I want to show two significantly different causes that people
share their negative influence. One is veiled love, and the other
is frustration and jealousy. I will provide a couple of unique
examples, and since I cannot tell your story, I will share mine.
The first is a tough decision to exclude negative family
members' influences, and the second is to overcome negativity
of strangers. I think you will understand the significance of each,
and perhaps find how this makes sense in your life.

Veiled Love of a Family

In the storm surrounding your life, it can be really hard to decide
on the best shelter. Some people will never decide on the right
shelter and perhaps choose to stand out in the middle of the
storm without any protection. The decisions we make can have a
lasting influence on the person we become, and some of them are
really difficult. If you avoid the tough decisions, you will often
also avoid a lot of rewards.

I have made some pretty outrageous choices in my life. I am sure
that you can think of a few pretty big ones you have made,
yourself. I want to share a series of decisions that made a huge
impact in my life, and I hope that you can either relate in some
way, or at least get a feel for this whole notion of living in the
storm instead of just waiting it out.

Living in the Storm

This is a story of a sacrifice I made that left me with nothing in the bank, an angry family, and a series of calamities that cost me some of the things that meant the most to me. The same sacrifice also took a turn that, upon later review, gave me all of the blessings I could ask for, and more.

I do not wish for a moment that you play a sad violin for me here. In fact, this is a good time to make the point that your pain and my pain are not different. We all feel the same pain, and hurt is relative to the person feeling it. While what I will tell is an example unique to me, it is also one that I suspect many people can relate to very easily. You may have a far more extreme example, and to that I would say that I only hope you will find a reason to gain inspiration on a similar scale to your pain.

I will give you some back-story, but you can make time for this. I hope you are comfortable and enjoying your read. Give me your trust that this gets to a point that you will appreciate.

In 2000, I met a woman. She was an extraordinary woman. She was a hard worker, creative, intelligent, and attractive in every way. She was a real jewel, and one of those people you would think of in the kindest terms. In fact, I cannot recall meeting a person who ever said a bad word about her. She came to know me for just the man I am … nothing more, and nothing less. We were fast friends, and soon became lovers. We were from very similar industries, and we had a lot in common, yet we also had a lot of differences in our backgrounds. She was educated, she came from a very cautious upbringing, and she was afraid to reach beyond her comfort zone.

In comes the knight in shining armor, of course. It was the battle-scarred businessman who had retired young, long enough to realize that was a bad idea, and was never afraid of risk. Yes, that is me. I had chased around the world for a few years as a young man, always hoping to find this brilliant young lady and create a family.

The woman is Peggy, and today she is my wife and mother of our three children. None of that came easy for either of us. We bent, and nearly broke, in order to merge two completely different personalities and risk profiles.

Peggy had a full-time job in middle-management in the banking industry, when one day she left work so disappointed by her career that I made a suggestion. I picked up the business card of her small company that she had considered her "other job" and I said, "Peggy, this is what you love to do, and it is what gives you the most joy. I think this is what you should be doing." She was nervous at the prospect, but by early 2001, we completed the merger of Peggy's company with my company. This was not just an emotional decision, but there were a lot of business considerations involved as well. We knew it would be a big challenge, but we were young and we felt up to it. Our plan was for her to keep her employment while I worked full-time to build our company.

Have you ever seen a storm cloud just before things start blowing hard and the waters rise into a flood? I have, and this was a storm about to cut loose in a major way. Peggy loved the dream ahead of us, but she was afraid of the sacrifice. I told her that I would work hard to make it happen, and I would let her know when it was time for her to give up her very traditional sense of security and make our new merger of companies her full-time effort. First, I had to show her reasons that it would be safe and secure for her.

Living in the Storm

Now, remember, I had been away from work for a few years, so I was a bit rusty, but I still had a few things rattling around in my old pre-thirties head. I also knew how to work very hard, and I never flinched at the hundred-plus hour per week schedule I kept. In fact, it was quite refreshing after having been a traveling bachelor. After all, I was doing this all for a great cause. I knew that I wanted to marry her and raise a family one day, and so I smiled with every small success our little company made.

One fateful day, we sat down and talked about the progress of our hard work. I told her that I needed her to spend more time with our company and less time with her middle-income security blanket that she called a job. Have you ever seen somebody utterly terrified of success? I did on that very day.

We cashed in all retirement funds, invested everything in our company, and faced the parents. Oh, yes, there were parents! When her mother and father met me and it was love at first sight. These people were awesome, and they felt the same about me. We sat and talked for hours. I became very close to her mother. In fact, I realized a lot more with every conversation we held, just how fortunate I was to happen upon such a truly kind family.

Our company hit a snag in late 2001, just as with many companies on September 11th. The fantasy was looking a bit bleak for a while. We had invested everything in our company and pushed it to the point of no return. We were already in too deep to give up. We spread our word far and wide and we had many advertisements both online and offline. We had our message in every publication we could afford, and all the while we invested very heavily in technology. How heavily did we invest? Let's just say that one hundred percent is the same thing for all of us. We took it to the limit.

We have always grown up to celebrate Christmas in our respective families. This is how we were raised, and it is what we came to know. By Christmas 2001, we had invested so heavily that we actually had a good amount of business coming in. We also had a lot of clients who also celebrated Christmas, and since a big economic upset in September, a lot of people were not paying their bill. We were an easy company to neglect, and as I said to Peggy, our Christmas gifts were sitting under our clients' trees. How bad was it? Well, we had a booming company with huge technology and marketing assets, but we counted on clients to pay us. We had sixty dollars in the bank, which was just enough to buy a Christmas tree and eat for a few more days until some people paid us. We did just that. We bought a beautiful tree, which was our gift to each other, and we decorated it with great pride. We still cherish the moment when we stood back in that huge empty room and gazed at our beautiful tree. Not to get ahead of myself, but that tree still means so much to us that each Christmas we adorn our home with seven fully decorated trees, two of which brush our home's ten foot ceilings, and each is decorated with the passion of two lovers. Our "Big Tree" in the living room takes a full ten hours to assemble.

Looking back, that must sound like a pretty shaky company, right? No, it was not. The company was doing great … you would perhaps even say that it was going gangbusters. The hardship was the separation of the company and the owners. We did not steal from our future. Instead, we toughed it out and had a very humble winter. We even had to borrow money to travel to see relatives. So you can surely imagine how that went over with Peggy's family. How do I say this properly and keep my language clean? Have you ever seen one of those nuclear test explosion videos? It was along those lines.

We felt pinned to the wall. We both had all the reasons to believe in our company, but we had an exposure to negativity from family that was out of nothing but love. Our parents were coming unglued, and nobody could blame them. We surely screwed things up, right? It got even more challenging. In fact, things got a whole lot worse, and fast.

We were in love. We had each other, for better or worse. We did not expect to have a family yet, but we were blessed with a baby on the way. Peggy was pregnant. We spent nearly five months loving our new discovery, choosing names, making plans, and we were always reminded of how fortunate we were. We knew that we would be great parents, and that because of our jobs in the Internet industry, we would often be able to work at home and spend time with our baby. In fact, having a family was the greatest reason we had worked so hard to build our company. We wanted the freedom to grow a family, and to do it on our terms.

Close to five months into the pregnancy, I got a call from Peggy saying that she was bleeding and she was heading to the hospital. I was frantic! I drove as fast as I could, with a dry mouth and racing pulse. It was one of those moments that takes all of your reality and throws it out the window.

When I got there and they performed a sonogram, the floor fell from beneath our feet. Our baby had not grown. They could not find a heartbeat. We lost our baby! Damn, do I really have to write this? Surely, you can imagine how this was for us. We are not alone. Many people endure this pain. To us, it was earth-shattering. Who was to blame? We had a huge amount of stress, so I took that on my shoulders. I assumed that Peggy blamed me, and she assumed that I blamed her. Then, we had more than one unnamed family member tell us that, because of our circumstances, it was for the best. No, not because the baby may have been unhealthy or because of some divine intervention … because of our *circumstances*! Have you ever seen your whole world turn red with anger and blue with sorrow at the same time? I think my head nearly exploded when I heard that, but at the same time, all I could do was to hold it in. I was the bad guy here, and I did not ever want to worsen my chances that our families would be at peace as one.

We found out that our baby was gone on a Friday, but it was the following Monday before Peggy endured a process called a DNC, which is how they removed our beloved child from her womb in a medical process. That was the worst weekend of our lives. Monday came, and I was every bit the man I could ever hope to be, but it was a hard time, and we barely knew how to speak afterward. It was so impossible to find the words for this sadness we shared. What do you say when your family is all of the sudden minus one person?

The doctor was kind, and he knew we would not understand it fully at the time, but he said that the best way we would heal from it would be when we come back again in a couple months with a new pregnancy. It was horrible to hear at the time, but that is exactly what we did.

We lived in Kansas City, which has dramatic seasonal changes. An ice storm hit our area that caused approximately 300,000 homes to be without power. It took linemen from across the USA to restore power to the city, and it was not a quick fix. An interesting fact of these storms is that exactly nine months later; the hospital maternity wards fill up. Maybe it is just a survival reflex, but when the power is out and people huddle in front of the fireplace to keep warm, people make babies. We did just that. It was our miracle baby, Simon. Although we still feel our love for the baby we lost, we are always reminded that Simon is our beloved miracle child. I say miracle, not only because he was the one who made us feel whole again, but because he was a very high-risk baby. The pregnancy nearly killed both Peggy and Simon. It would have, if not for a stroke of very good medical attention during the pregnancy.

Onward and stormward, we continued our pursuit. With Simon growing inside Peggy each day, it came time that we had to make a court appearance. Sure, business was booming, but we had recently made the decision to invest in the needed technology to take on a new venture. We had a new client who courted us, and we also had a lot of receivables to collect. We just did not have the income we believed to be necessary to pay ourselves a reasonable salary. So we are bad at business, right? Well, not really, but it did land us in court, where we were ordered out of our home. We walked; well actually, Peggy waddled because she was eight months pregnant, to the front of the room. The judge said something, but all we heard was "Get out!"

Oh crap! How will we explain this to the families? Somebody is surely going to hang my head on the wall for this calamity. A well-intentioned and presumably successful businessman with a booming company certainly cannot have an eight month pregnant wife without a place to rest. Clearly I am a real bad guy. There is no other answer.

We moved to Topeka, where we already had an office building and to-be-grandparents to our new baby nearby. We found a terrible little home within a city block of the school where I spent my last days of formal education.

We spent four months in that miserable little hell hole, and then moved to a very lovely home that we were very proud of. Things had made a swift turn for us, just as we had carefully calculated. It was very challenging, but we made the sacrifices we knew were necessary to reach our goals. Such is business, and such is life.

Her family did not forgive us for their stress. They were so angry for the worries we imposed upon them, that they totally lost sight of the fact we were fearlessly living our lives and rising above the storm. At times, it felt as if they were angry with us for trying to reach our dreams and that they would be much happier to see us only live up to their goals, and their reality. Some of them were downright hateful toward me. Peggy had cousins who did not have anything but a message that their cousin Peggy was involved with some awful guy who was destroying her life and making her poor. So how can I defend that? Sure, we went broke for a short number of months, only to have a cash flow that would choke even the biggest of horses a few months later. Yet, I was still the biggest creep on the planet to some of her family.

One day it all came together for a perfect storm. It was a family Easter celebration. Much of her father's side of the family was there. Peggy's brother was really quite defensive of his older sister. This was interesting, because from all I ever heard from her over the years was that she was delighted when he had more than a sentence to speak to her. In this case, it was to be the instance he would make that all up to her and defend her for all of those times he neglected her presence.

Our son, Simon was very young, and we apparently did not have enough diapers with us. While I was entertaining some of the little kids, Peggy slipped out to pick up more diapers at her parents' home nearby. By the time she returned, hell was in full fury, and her husband was under attack.

We were sitting in a large banquet room full of family, when I apparently got to be too much for her brother. He stood up and flipped the entire table on me, and others on my side of the table. Then he jumped over the pile of ham, deviled eggs, and other Easter favorites to physically attack me. Oh, it was a beauty! We had Mark in one corner, and the entire family lynch mob in the other corner. I really thought I was in the hottest corner of hell for a while. We really had it out, and I was physically attacked like I was some animal. It was not pretty. All that time, I refused to take a swing. I just knew that if I so much as made even the slightest defensive move that I would lose all respect from my wife and I would be out of there forever. The worst I did was that as I was smothered under a pile of men trying to restrain her brother, I bit him on his side. I literally was about to go dark from being smothered, so I bit … not a little bite, but I bit with a fury that only comes from being afraid I may not get another breath!

Peggy returned to find this hell-storm, and she was pissed! I do not mean in the European drunk sort of pissed … she was angry with an unbridled fury that I only imagined could come from 50 women! I have to admit, I was a whole lot more afraid of her than the mob of her defenders swarming around me like angry hyenas.

I knew the screaming would come soon. In fact, I think the whole angry mob was scared to death of what was about to be unleashed from Peggy. It was like time stood still when she swung open the door to find this unexpected attack.

She spoke as eloquently as I think I have ever heard her speak. It was at a pinnacle of anger, but yet, quite eloquent. I think she perhaps would not have said it better if she rehearsed it for weeks. She really belted it out with a pride and dedication to her family that I could never have expected. The family that she was dedicated to was me! I thought for sure that somehow I was going to be put on a spit and roasted over the fire, but she walked into that place, said her piece, walked out with me, and did not speak to a single person in that room for many months. Years later, she has still not spoken to most of them.

We left there shaking with anger and fear. She drove the 170 miles back to our home, and the whole time she was furious with her family. She had told them that regardless of anything they thought they knew of me that I was many times the man any of them ever hoped or dared to be. She explained that although they had it out for me because we had financial challenges, that it was a mutual decision we had made as husband and wife. She also reminded her parents what they had known about my many past successes they had been so enamored by when they met me, and that the reason we had invested everything was based on that same experience. It was really a beautiful speech. It was also the speech that changed my life more than any other … before or since!

Peggy really made her stand. Her mother and father called many times, month after month, and Peggy would refuse to take the calls. This was not only because she was filled with anger, but after a while, it was because she had come to thoroughly enjoy a new life without any of the negativity or criticisms that she had received for so long. She was completely unwilling to hear anything that would bring her down. After all, before that day, she had never looked at me with totally untainted eyes and seen how much love we had to share. Once she was making her own clear decisions, she loved it, and she was not about to go back to the old standard.

The next time she spoke to her mother and father was only after Peggy knew she had more positivity in her life than anybody, even her relentlessly cynical mother, could tarnish. The first conversation included news that she would be having a new baby soon, and that we were planning to move into our new custom built home.

Strangely, once her mother saw that things were amazing for us, she told me that I was an alright guy after all. She actually started to treat me with respect again. She stopped telling Peggy she was better off without me, and she would actually hold a conversation with me again. Although we allow Peggy's mother in our lives today, we express caution at every turn, because her pessimism is so pervasive that we must frequently realize how much it diminishes our growth as a family.

I do not wish to tell others to break away from family members or to send away old friends. I would simply suggest taking inventory of those who will help you to see a brighter side of life, and those who create conflict and confusion. Those who crush your dreams in the name of love are still crushing your dreams all the same. Many will do so with the best intentions, but even the best intentions can become very destructive. Make your stand, fortify your position, and make the right decisions for you.

In our instance, weeding out the negativity propelled our marriage into a joy that we would have previously never imagined. It created a successful environment that would boost all other efforts in our lives to unbelievable new heights. We made more friends, our business skyrocketed, and we found life above the storm.

Strangers Who Hurt You

We have considered how much a loved one can hurt you. The ones you trust and respect have more power to hurt you than any other. Whether it is a parent, a high school guidance counselor, or a friend, those people with a seemingly qualified opinion can deliver a destructive message better than any other.

Now I want to show you an example of how a jealous stranger can, and will, hurt you if you allow them. If you do not already have experiences that remind you who to hold dear, maybe this one will help to remind you who to hear and who to tune out. In this case, I will use a story that is very fresh in my mind.

I recently released a book titled *"Twitter for Business: Twitter for Friends"*. It covered many topics on the use of the Internet social media Website, Twitter.com, and the importance of building social media relationships. I discussed uses of social media from both business and personal perspectives, with an attempt to bridge a gap between the two. After all, the value of the people is the greatest asset for a company, and when those people feel a part of a company, and carry a personal responsibility and accountability for their role, the business becomes a whole lot more tasteful. People want to reach out to people, and they want to connect. I think I shared a lot of great insight from a position of experience. I have been in business for a couple decades, I have used Twitter enough to write a book about it, and I did it all with a good intention of helping people. So what could be so wrong about that?

After the release of the book, I received much support from friends and strangers alike, but there was also criticism. When you write a book about a hot topic, some people will assume a negative position that you just did it to cash in on a new craze.

Their cynicism kicks into overdrive, and they cannot imagine that you would do something to be helpful. Sure, some royalties would be great, but writing books, for me, has a lot more to do with passion than "cashing in". It is not as easy as it looks, and most of the hundreds of thousands of books released each year will sell fewer than five hundred copies. The assumption of cashing in is pretty far-fetched. Although I really believe that anything can happen, and I believe in dreams coming true, I also understand mathematics.

In some cynics' minds, if you are doing it to be helpful, it should be given for free and there should be no remuneration for the work. I believe that if you do enough good things for others without unreasonable expectations of reward, the reward takes on a different measurement. The greatest reward for me was internal. I know that I did the right thing. I know that even if I do not help on the scale I hope for, I still help. I may even make a huge change in somebody's life. I may help a company to stay in business and save somebody's job. I may help somebody to meet their spouse. I may make an impact! If this is the case, I think it is only fair that the cost of my time is covered, and that I should earn my small book royalties. To the cynic, that may seem unreasonable.

I spent hundreds of hours during a time that my company and my family needed me very much. My company took on some huge losses last year, and we welcomed the birth of our third child during the production of that book. I knew that I would not have a big budget to market it, but I took it on faith that it would be useful enough that people would talk about it. How do you criticize that?

If you put your heart out there, it is an easy welcome for attack. One such attack was from a cynic who has proven his jealousy of me in so many instances that my wife has posed the concern of when we will find this guy peeking in our windows. I mean, this guy seems to follow my every move, and he tries to find every reason that he can insult or hurt me. You may wonder what I have done to this person, and I wonder the same thing. I have never met him. He is just that type of person who seeks power in negativity. You surely know the type. This is my best example of a stalker. It is also the person who will attempt to use the power of negativity to sway others. It is a truly damning person to allow influence in your life. You may not have a stalker, but I am sure you can point out somebody who makes you uncomfortable by their negativity. Then, you find the ones you can count on without a doubt.

Now, I want to give you the reverse. I want to share a completely opposite view. On Saturday, just a few days ago, I took my family to an event that happened to be held next door to the last school I attended as a kid. That school was a horrible place where they sent the "bad" kids. Just driving by it reminded me of some horrific things I saw in the years I was there. I saw kids who would cut on themselves, and not always just for attention, but some of them truly wanted to die … some achieved it. The school was set on the grounds of Topeka State Hospital, which was a state operated mental hospital. It included kids from the local school district, and it was also where mental patients living at the state hospital would attend school if they received enough merits to be in school. Some were surely some decent kids who just got lost, and others were violent criminals. I was there because nobody knew what to do with me, and I was a pretty hard nut to crack. I walked into that school with a foot high black Mohawk, black nail polish, black lipstick, a chain running from one of my ears into my pierced nose, a black leather trench coat, and a kid behind it that was so confused about life that no wardrobe could define it.

Since we were so close to the school, I drove through the school grounds. As we drove away was when I asked my dear wife Peggy how she would feel if I wrote another book back-to-back with my last release, which has still not taken off yet. Before I give you her statement, which should be apparent by now since I am clearly writing the book, I will tell you more about this horrible storm that made me stronger.

I was sent to this school after having missed more school than I attended from age ten through age thirteen. I was a real truancy problem for the school system. I actually skipped more school from the time I was in sixth grade, until the time I made my final leave from school, than I attended. According to common standards, it is a wonder that I am not dead or in jail.

The school system really tried to work with me the best they knew how. In fact, they ended up awarding me three grade promotions because, according to my age, I was about three years behind my class. After all, I did not technically pass a grade since sixth grade. They would give me a pre-test, a few papers to write, a post-test, and voila … I passed another grade. This was not common, but this was a different sort of school, and not a standard part of the educational system of the time.

I guess they really had a problem with sending a kid out into the world with a transcript that showed a sixth grade education. I think that was noble of them, in their selfish way of defending their jobs.

I was very wary of school, because I always realized that school largely teaches *what* to think, while making little or no consideration of *how* to think. Independent thinking is discouraged, thus I was not their ideal pupil. I was a true misfit in their agenda.

I made my final leave from formal education shortly after my fifteenth birthday. Of course, this was not without the courts involved. I was in and out of court enough that my mother actually changed her name back to her maiden name because she was so tired of seeing the name Murnahan in the newspaper.

So how does this story show the power of love beating jealousy? Peggy made a statement that made me absolutely confident in my request to write another book, even though it could jeopardize our family's security and create a burden for each of us. She said, "I know the book you will write, Mark, and I know it will change some lives." That was enough for me. She had once again proved that doing the right thing, even in the midst of a storm, is just the right thing to do. Good people cannot avoid it, and even bad people sometimes cannot avoid doing the right things.

I am glad that I took Peggy's inspiration instead of listening to that jealous antagonist. I hope you are glad as well.

Create a Cheering Section

Who cares about you? This is a question that we must evaluate, and reevaluate from time to time. I shared how those who care about you, including family, will not always provide the best influence, but they still hold a high importance in your life. A challenge can be found in how to win them over and to create a cheering section. If you can do it, the results of that encouragement can be hard to measure.

A good way to start a cheering section is by encouraging the hopes and desires of others and being a fan. Sometimes those hopes are simple to uncover, and sometimes they require some extra fact-finding. People's motivations are not always clear, and a lot of people will never share them for fear of rejection. I mean, if I told my wife that I want to be a rock singer, she would fall out of her chair laughing. However, if she thought I meant it, and I really wanted to make a go of it, the laughter may turn to fear. I have no desire to sing, but I love to write books, and I love to race cars. When it comes to those around you, do you know what they want? Sometimes it goes beyond just listening and you must ask questions. When you know what *others* want, it may make the things *you* want seem a whole lot more attainable than you ever thought. It can also be much easier to be their fan, and help cheer them on toward their goals.

I consider the low-carbohydrate diet I am on as a way to be a fan. I am doing it for two important motivations. One reason is because I want to lower my cholesterol and triglycerides. Well, actually, my wife wants me to lower my cholesterol and triglycerides, but she makes a good case for it. The far more important reason is that I am giving support for my wife as she works to lose weight leftover from her recent pregnancy. I know her motivation, and I support her. I am her cheering section.

I have friends who are elected officials. That is not a goal for me in the least. It is their goal, and I am always happy to put up yard signs to help them reach their goals. That is an obvious goal, and never hidden. On the other hand, if a friend has a goal of getting their deck stained over the weekend, it is often not as obvious. Being a fan can mean being aware of changing goals.

There are many unknown aspirations of those around you. Knowing the motivations of others and finding out how you can help is a great way to rally them. It will make you feel good to do it. It will also often prompt people to wonder about your goals. They may or may not already know what you want in life. Share these things with friends, and build a support network. The best way to begin is by giving to others and becoming one of those altruistic people you admire. Even if you are already doing it, do it more.

I recall a story that happened between two old friends. Mike was selling his home and upgrading to a new home. John was the number one real estate agent in town. Mike asked John to help him price the home for sale. These guys have been friends for quite some time, and John was really good at his work. It seemed natural that Mike would count on John to list his home. Mike took the value John gave him and went to a complete stranger to list his home for sale. That was Mike's decision, and John certainly did not count on the commission from selling the house. It still bothered John, and does to this day, that his long-time friend did not give him the consideration. It was not a matter of listing fees, because John would have probably sold it without charging him anything. Mike later said that the only reason he had called the other agent was that he thought she was good looking. He was a single guy … go figure.

When you are not a fan of your friends, can you really expect them to be your fan? This is not to say that anybody owes anybody, but if it came time for John to need Mike's services, I can imagine he will remember that lack of loyalty.

Mike was once a great inspiration to me, and I sat in his cheering section, as did John. In fact, it seemed that he had a lot of loyal fans. Time and again, we watched as Mike neglected other friends and cared for his own goals, but never those of others. Neither of us communicates with Mike much these days, and we have heard many mutual friends say similar things about him. It is sad to see his fans leave the bleachers, but it is easy to understand why.

When you treat friends with the kindness of helping them achieve their goals or by inspiring them, you are a huge step toward gaining another fan in your cheering section. We all need as many of those as we can get. Do not forget to cheer on your friends.

Some people will never be a fan. My mother-in-law was in town this weekend, and I asked if she would give her perspective on the latest book I am working on. She said "Sure". Well, first, she said "No, I don't want to read anything about Twitter", but I explained that was a different book, and that this one was more up her alley. I gave her a part that there could surely be no negativity over. I was actually just curious if I could reach a real pessimist with a little dose of optimism.

She read about fifteen pages and said that it seems "too autobiographical" and went on to say "Coming from a guy your age that seems arrogant". I tried to gather a couple of thoughts, but the most important one that readily came to mind was that this cynical old lady has done less to inspire others in her sixty-some years than I did by the time I was out of diapers. She has never taken a risk, and she discourages others from doing the same. She has never really achieved much joy in life; she hates her job and nearly everything else around her. I could have thrown my 37 years of experience around, but then I would have just as well thrown it in the trash before I would reach this woman. If age was her real concern, she is missing out on some really great lessons that can be taken from others. I learn from my young children every day.

Did I tell her this at the time? No, because I really do not need to lose sleep over a fan that will never be. The point is to choose your cheering section well. Give everybody the opportunity, but remember that you cannot win them all.

An interesting observation that you may notice about my mother-in-law and the story of Mike and John is that sometimes the people close to you will underestimate your real value more than a stranger will. This is also a good reminder to look closer at those around you to be sure that you are not underestimating them, too.

The One with Thick Glasses

I have seen this scene played out in many movies and also in real life, so I hope you can relate to this. I want you to imagine the scene of three young ladies out on the town on a Saturday night. Their relationship has a hierarchy. There is the really pretty one, the in-between one, and then the one with thick glasses and braces. In a different version of this scene, I want to encourage you to spread your time between the roles of each, in hope that you may find value in being the one with thick glasses.

Put aside all negative considerations of social climbing and take a look at the people around you. Some are the people that help you feel better because you perceive that they do not have it as good as you. It makes you the pretty one to be around this person. You may feel better about yourself and your life by contrasting it with the self-esteem or the life of this less fortunate friend. You are "the pretty one" and they are "the one with thick glasses". In reality, if you are to be the pretty one, and this is truly your friend, you will serve them best by being an inspiration to them. The pretty one should never seek joy from the disadvantage or the troubles of others in their life. The one with thick glasses may look up to you for reasons you never realized. Rather than considering how they make you feel better by contrast to their life, consider their point of view and create reasons that they may genuinely admire you. In many relationships, you may find yourself as both the pretty one and the one with thick glasses. You can learn a lot from each other.

Other friends will create a feeling somewhere in between, and are just down to earth people, like you. You enjoy your time with them because you feel a common ground. This is a great kind of friend.

Being the one with thick glasses can mean that you will choose to spend time with others who inspire you. That means you spend time with the pretty one, but never the kind who gains joy in their superiority. I mean the kind of person that inspires you and you look at with a reverence for the great person they are. This pretty one makes you feel good just to know them. They are somebody you want to introduce to people as your friend, because you think everybody should know somebody this kind, caring, and inspiring.

If you take more time to be the one in thick glasses, and spend time with those people who inspire the best in you, it is easy to see how you can be the pretty one to more people around you, and for all the right reasons.

Spread your time in each role, and start enjoying being the one with thick glasses. If you will make more efforts to spend time with those who inspire you, it is likely to find that you also inspire them. This mutual inspiration creates a synergy that should never be underestimated.

Family Breakdown

Times are changing fast and it may sometimes feel like the world is spinning out of control. Parents of all ages have claimed the troubles of "kids these days". Some have claimed that "these are the worst of times". People have likely said these things for centuries, but let's look at some of the changes, and consider some possible shortcomings in our adaptation.

I have written about being selective of who you spend your time and attention with. I even told a story of severing negative family ties. Of course, this is not to be the standard. Family is a precious resource that is very often neglected and taken for granted. I also wrote of inviting family into your cheering section and winning them over. This is preferred, whenever it is possible.

Necessity or Negligence

I am not the first person that you have found expressing a concern of family values. Deterioration of families is a widespread epidemic that is often very pronounced in Western culture. As people found more things that they "needed" such as color television, air conditioning, and two automobiles, that feeling of need grew greater. Those "needs" of yesteryear sprung into demands for larger homes, fancier cars, cellular phones for each child over the age of seven, and a lifestyle that every neighbor would envy. The rat race was on, and the forces of peer pressure took men and women by the nose and led them away from their families.

I am not only addressing Western society, so do not mistake this. The closeness of families is a worldwide concern, and the epidemic is spreading. When people drift away from families, they also drift away from much of the positive nurturing that only a family can provide.

I have witnessed cultures from all around the world, and the precious demand for more hours in the day is not exclusive to any nation. More than anywhere else, I find that many of the swift changes in American society have fallen tragically short of the joys that were expected by the changes. We have thrown ourselves into so many changes that our adaptations have often been made in haste.

Consider this common acceptance of cultural failure in the past couple decades, and question whether it is based on necessity or negligence. As families accepted both parents working, daycares and schools were left to raise the kids. As parents took second and third jobs, the family suffered further demise. Kids are often left to raise themselves, and each other. I see this every day, even in my insulated upper-middle-class cocoon. Kids are off on their own, or in groups of other kids who may or may not be a good influence. That influence often goes unmonitored while parents' communication is limited to the time they wake up and the time they go to bed, perhaps with a few text messages in between. I am not saying that this is the standard. I will say, however, that it is prevalent enough to warrant parents' attention. As a chorus, we all say "not my kid", but just remember that it is *somebody's* kid who will bring a gun to school or teach your kids to use drugs. Their parents probably do not expect it either.

Living in the Storm

As the work-related pressures add up, parents communicate less, kids become more troubled, and the family breaks down. Before you know it, they give it all up for divorce and try over with a whole new dynamic. Does any of this sound familiar?

In such a self-indulgent society, we do what feels good for the moment and then we expect our children to learn from that example. When it all comes undone and it is too late to take it back and start over, we just hope that our kids will do better than we did.

Stop it! **You** do better, and **you** teach them right. Now is the best time to set a legacy into action. If you do not provide the best example now, then you really have neglected your family. Family should never be subjected to living here and now and doing what feels good for the moment, without weighing it in favor of what is best in the future. This kind of neglect is far too popular, and it is usually bred of despair. Family is the genesis of all society. We all come from somewhere, and we learn most of our best and worst lessons as a result of how we were raised within our family. If you worry for society, be mindful that it starts with the responsibility and dedication of each family.

Whether you are the kid in this scenario, a spouse, a grandparent, or just a curious onlooker, I hope you will share your time and share support to prevent the breakdown. If you feel that you have already been sucked into this tornado-like storm, please take the care to remember the things that once made your family happy and positive about your future. Make a commitment to needed adjustments to prevent the breakdown. Sometimes dedication to an old standard of sitting together for dinner is enough to improve the dialogue within a family. It sounds so simple, but yet it is one of the first things to blow away in the storm.

Take the time to express yourself, and do not wait another day!

For the Single Mother or Father

Living as a single parent is challenging, but apparently quite possible. It surely must seem impossible at times, but greater than thirteen million single parents are raising over twenty one million children in USA alone. Recent census estimates reflect approximately twenty six percent of children in USA today are raised in a single parent home. With such astonishing numbers, it is obviously not only possible, but common.

If you are a single parent and things seem to always be a mess, please be reminded that you are not alone. Be very mindful of creating joy and inspiration for yourself and others. Your family needs you to be strong. You already know this in great abundance. I have seldom seen a single parent without the drive to succeed, or willingness to sacrifice. Remain strong and make good decisions.

If there is another parent in the equation, do not let any child grow to see them as a monster, even if you deeply believe that they are. It is easy to hold anger, but when the anger is directed toward somebody with a permanent role of influence; this only serves to harm a child's self esteem. Just imagine how hard it is to grow up living two completely different lives in disagreement, each in conflict with the other. In one life, it is accepted to love mommy, and in the other life it is accepted to love daddy. When the two lives collide within the heart and mind of the child, the confusing and painful outcome is something that neither parent would wish upon their child. Patience and love for a child is often not enough to override the anger of a scorn person, but for the child's best interest you must find forgiveness and respect. It is a lot easier to say than to put into action, but you must be ready for the challenge in order to provide the best for the child. Do your best to show your love and compassion for the child by finding forgiveness and understanding of the other parent. Your child needs you and deserves your very best.

One of the worst things I have ever witnessed from single parents is a pressing desire to find that missing link … another parent. I can imagine that this is a reaction of many single parents at some point in their life. It is hard to be alone, and everybody deserves somebody. I may not have a magic pill for this, but I would like to encourage you. Creating joy and inspiration in your own life is the first step. Finding harmony with the family you have should always come before introducing another. Most people know this, but neglecting it due to loneliness, convenience, security, or other reasons is also a very common mistake. I have been that add-on man, and I will always regret the confusion it must have caused for the children.

Breaking a Cycle

Some cycles are hard to break and may even seem impossible to overcome. There is so much science that tells us what we are and who we are expected to be that it should be impossible to break away. Tragically, instead of accepting the cycle to be broken, many people will hide in shame of their lineage or their culture of negativity instead of deciding to stop it.

It is time to consider the impossible. Who others expect you to be can crush you, but only if you allow it. Be reminded that their doubts in you are their own, and far less important than what you expect of yourself. Exceptions to science and society's expectations occur each and every day. I will share a couple of impossibilities with you and let you imagine how this may fit into your life. I want you to consider the pride of breaking a negative cycle in comparison to continuing it. Sometimes the cycle is no worse than chasing a dream that a parent was too cautious to pursue, and sometimes it is a matter of coming from a horrific upbringing. Whatever the case, consider your cycle, and how you will improve it.

My father was one tough guy. He was raised during "The Great Depression". I have wondered why they used the word "great", but I think I found a few answers. I think there are some lessons that really were great about it. It taught people to pull together.

They were forced to work with their neighbors. It took a lot from people, but what it gave back were some lessons that will far outlast the pains. Perhaps some similar lessons are occurring again today.

A lesson of caring that stands out in my mind is one in which my father was walking home from school as a little boy in the 1930's and found a beautiful porcelain teacup in an alley. The handle was broken off, but it was beautiful to him. He had watched his mother and step-father being broken down by the economy and loss of their worldly possessions, so he tried to make it all feel better for his Mommy. He took that broken teacup home to her with hopes of helping her feel happy with his little gift of beauty. It may not seem like a lot to some people, but to me, I imagine this little boy's hopes of cheering up his Mommy, and I imagine how she cried.

This seems like a pretty kind cycle, and one that should not be broken. The other side of the coin is the cycle he had to break, which is much gloomier. It reminds me to weigh everything carefully, and that we can occasionally learn as much from evil as we can from good, by recognizing who we refuse to become.

My father was raised by a mother and stepfather while his drunkard pedophile biological father rotted in a prison and was later found dead in an alley. He was in and out of jail most of his life. I did not find out about it until long after my father's death, but his dad was a really tormented and sick soul. Although my father did many great things to influence others in very positive ways, I also had a cycle to break. Between the two generations, I found enough disgust that it forced me to try even harder to break the cycle. Each generation taught lessons to the next, and the ugly cycle came undone.

Never Remain a Victim

My father was not an alcoholic or pedophile, but he was horribly abusive to my mother. I remember a time as a child when he took me and two of my brothers to his ex-wife's house for the night. He had been having a fight with my mother and he wanted to be sure we were not there to witness it.

He was often a very insecure man. My mother held excuses for him such as his chronic pain from osteoarthritis that begun when he was injured during World War II, the medications, or that he was 21 years older than her and worried that other men desired her. The truth was that he had a sickness.

On the night he took us out of our beds for a two hour ride to his ex-wife's home, he had a lot of time to think. It was a long drive back home to my mother, and a sane person would think that it gave him time to reflect. His reflection was on the anger and frustration he felt. He returned home to relentlessly beat my mother until her eyes were swollen and filled with blood. He then brandished a handgun and as she lay on the bed in horror, he fired shots on each side of her head as he screamed at her with fury. It is truly a wonder that I was not orphaned that night, or many others like it, by a sick man in a rage.

The madness continued, and although he was not as brutal to me, I can recall much horror that he caused my older brother David. Dad was relentless, and he always seemed to have it out for David. In fact, early on the day of my father's death, he testified against David in a court claim that he had stolen some collectables from dad. Only a few hours later, while I was home watching television with David, two of our brothers walked in to deliver the news that dad was gone. He had died in a car crash that would always be suspected as suicide.

When I look back at my childhood, I never did see myself as a victim. Of course, if I saw somebody screaming at three young boys for being "selfish little bastards" and making them pick dandelions from the yard for their dinner, I would call that abusive. Now that I put it down on paper, I guess I had some pretty insane encounters. I dealt with some pretty messed up stuff. More than I will include in this book.

Something important to consider when you look at where you have been is just how many stories of a happier life you hear that have come from self-pity. I really cannot imagine anything good that can come from feeling like a victim. There are things to learn from it, but if you wallow in pity instead of rising above it, you will become a victim of nobody but yourself.

In contrast to being a victim, we often hear stories of success that come from rising above expectations. Those who walk through tragedy and receive it as a valuable lesson are no longer victims. They remind us that even the worst atrocity can create something better. The tragedy may always be there, but the value received outweighs the negative.

Let us look at this in another light. We call people who survive cancer "survivors" because of a pronounced and significant responsibility that they have of sharing their optimism and spirit for life with others. They were once considered victims. When they spoke up with a huge benefit of inspiring others, they strongly renounced the title of "victim" and are now a huge force of possibility and producers of greatness.

Everybody who became truly great has traveled through the storm and shows testament to the value of overcoming obstacles and inspiring others to do the same. **They are never victims!**

It does not take a traumatic instance in your life to receive a lesson. As I stated before, sometimes the cycle is no worse than chasing a dream that a parent was too cautious to pursue. Maybe the challenge is only to become stronger than you were yesterday. Whatever the case, do not be a victim.

We each have tragedies, and they all hurt. How we choose to deal with the tragedy will determine what we can do with it, and who we become.

Justified Failure

I have heard a lot of excuses from people for their failures. Some people justify their failure, and others will choose to never even try to succeed at achieving the life they want. Some wildly popular excuses that I have heard for failure include where they were raised, education, upbringing, race, genetically-imposed expectations, physical handicaps, economy, and more. The list can go on seemingly forever with excuses. These excuses help people to justify their failure, but how can that be justified? The list of people who have overcome these obstacles and much bigger challenges and subsequently become legendary proves these excuses to be invalid. The person with excuses for failure makes it impossible to succeed. If you have made excuses to justify your failure, that is over!

If you are smart enough to read this page, then you are smart enough to win in your life. You are smart enough to overcome your obstacles and use them for strength. You are smart enough to understand that being the victim will never give you what you really seek. Some people would say that is it easier to be a victim than a survivor. That may be true in some ways, but the lengthier outcome of being a victim has got to be a truly terrible life.

They Are Only Words

They are only words, but it comes all too often that they are easy to take to heart. Don't do it! Do not buy into other's hate. Remember that they only use mean words because they cannot find a better way to hurt you or steal your hopes. They are the weak ones seeking an upper hand in any way they can find it, and hurting you is proof that they can beat you.

If you find that you are more offended by words like jerk, creep, fag, queer, dummy, shorty, fatass, idiot, moron, nigger, chink, coolie, gook, wap, spic, beaner, hymie, kike, bog, or others, than you are inspired to overcome and conquer these despicable standards of hatred and demoralization, then you may as well accept them. When you accept the values of hatred and anger into your life, then you are diminishing your potential and being a victim. Many of the greatest leaders and admired people of all time heard these words of hatred and many more. Did it hurt them? Sure, it probably did for a while, but then they made a decision to overcome the anger and pain.

Take a minute and think of the worst things people have ever said to you. Get upset, be absolutely furious, and cry if you need to. Then, when you are done feeling whatever it is that you have to get out, make a decision that from this day forward you will not hear these things. Let there be no concern for retaliation, no revenge, no anger, **nothing!** Let them say what they will. They are now the weaker ones. You have taken away their power, and you are the one who will win!

Live Without Fear

Do not be afraid of disappointment. If you do not create a risk, you stand very little to gain. I have three kids, and I know they will let me down in some ways, at times. The reward is worth the risk.

If you really value fear, try these on for size: Consider the fear of missed opportunities for joy in your life. Consider the fear of having a life that is not your own, or that is not what you wanted. With these fears, the worst outcomes are often made real by failing to create any risk in your life. Although fear can save your life, it can also make it far less enjoyable. Surely you have heard the old saying, "Nothing ventured, nothing gained."

What is worth a risk for you? I would not say that it is a good idea to pack up and leave your family to start a budding career as a rock singer. I do not mean risks that are outrageous or foolhardy. Then again, what is outrageous and foolhardy for some, is not so risky for others. We all have our own threshold for risk. I believe that it is important to analyze it from time to time and decide if it is outdated or still useful. Maybe it needs revamping in order to match new circumstances.

I can certainly give you a good example of overcoming fear and taking risks. When I decided to write a book earlier this year, I knew the risk was steep. I had a lot of fears to face. Would it be useful to others, or would I just be laughed at? Would it ever sell more than fourteen copies? Believe me, this author gig is scary … especially the thought of making it a full-time job and doing it for an income. I took the risk head on, and I battled through a whole lot of doubts. I still have doubts in sales performance, but I know that some people will like the work. The reward of a job well done helps me along. I know that some people have received a benefit from the work, and I have created my cheering section that helps to keep me excited.

Shortly after that book was released, I realized that there was a whole lot more passion to write. So I am taking on yet another big risk, and you are reading it right now. If I have created some inspiration in your life, I have done my job well. I consider it a great reward.

I have learned that fears rooted in self-doubts are commonly more destructive than positive. I plug right along at the keyboard and push through those fears. I hope that you will decide to do the same, and remember the benefit of taking a few risks of your own.

What will your risk be, and what will get in your way?

Ideas Without Action

Great ideas are not so hard to come by, but putting them into action takes dedication. Consider how many times you have thought of something brilliant, only to let that idea go idle. That idea may be to spend more time with family, enjoying a hobby, or turning your passion into a business. Whatever the idea, it will not happen without action. A tragic outcome for many great ideas is that they get wrapped in doubts and excuses and never reach their potential.

There is only one person to blame. The good news is that the person to blame is also the person who gets to take much of the credit when action is taken. Beginning today I want you to try a more productive approach. When you have an idea, write it down, make a decision, and create an action plan.

Live Long-Term

A common reason that ideas go stagnant is a feeling that there is just not enough time in the day, week, or month. Life is already busy, and adding another task seems daunting. It means that something must go, and it can seem hard to sacrifice one thing for another. Scheduling gets tight, and goals go undone. I know what it is like. I imagine how many sticky notes I have wasted by jotting down ideas that somehow end up in a desk drawer and eventually into the paper shredder. The shredder is a tragic end for many great plans, and those are just the lucky ones that made it to ink and paper. Some plans will make it past the sticky note and into action, but then the effort gets overwhelming and after pulling out a lot of hair, the extra headache warrants a break. The break ends up lasting longer, and before long, the whole idea is gone. Maybe the idea is revisited later, but the memory of all of those doubts come back, and often do not make up for the initial enthusiasm. All of the sudden it just looks like another drain of your time. Does this sound familiar to you?

Time is not wasted when the plan is implemented. Time is only wasted when you give up. It is an investment, similar to the stock market. When you invest in the stock market, the money is not lost until you turn your shares back into money by selling them at the wrong time. You may still lose a lot of your time with an idea, but the worst loss happens when you give up early and cash in at a low time. Like any investment, a long-term approach can provide a lower risk of loss. Making long-terms goals and an action plan that will sustain the test of time takes long-term vision. Expecting the unexpected and keeping enthusiasm amidst your doubts takes conviction.

If you have an idea, whatever the idea, seeing it to completion is a lot easier when you take careful inventory of your life and find a place to fit it into your existing plans. When taking inventory, you must provision resources and the most valuable being time. Shifting other goals and ideas to shorter-term completion or longer-term completion is often necessary. When you take inventory and plan carefully with a far-sighted approach addressing the vision of what you want down the road, you are a lot more likely to achieve it than looking short-term and giving up when it does not happen on your timeframe.

Keeping Score

Keeping score can have some pretty bad uses. If you keep score of a person's wrong deeds against you, it can certainly create a grudge. Keeping score of your own deeds, on the other hand, can be a great step toward being better than ever. Simply writing it down and having a reference point could be enough to show you how much better you are than you perhaps ever knew. It can also show areas you would like to improve, and give you a clearer picture of how others see you.

You did not think that "Living in the Storm" would be simple, did you? No, it will take work, and I am going to ask you to perform some tasks. I think you will consider these some really easy tasks, and I think you will likely see a lot of benefit. This will not take the skill of a rocket scientist, brain surgeon, or a *rocket surgeon*. You can do this, and since I know how busy it can get in the storm of life, I am not going to ask you to spend a huge amount of time.

This is not for me, this is for *you*. If you start to feel doubtful, please just question what you have to lose, and if necessary, go back and re-read what I wrote about cynicism. I want you to simply try this for two weeks. If that works out, keep going and try it for a month. First, we will work in small steps. I do not want to ask too much, so let's see some improvement before we get carried away with a big commitment to improvement. That seems fair, doesn't it? If I am wrong, you can wad it all up in a ball and throw it at me.

Create Your Lists and Keep Them Near

I challenge you to keep a very basic diary of your progress. This will not be too much work, so I want you to give it your best effort. I will provide much of the work for you in the very tail end of this book, where you will find the lists I am asking you to keep. I will also give you a method to score your efforts in the next couple weeks on your own honor.

I will not be looking over your shoulder, but I want to be there in book form within your reach to remind you and encourage you to take this inventory of your actions, if you will allow me. I want you to keep this book with you, whether it is in your briefcase, purse, backpack, laptop case, or wherever you will find it handy when you need to add to your lists.

Reasons for Pride

First, I want you to make a list of things that you do each day that make you feel proud of yourself. This could be when you do something nice for somebody else, something that you would put on a résumé, or the type of thing you would want others to remember you by after you are long gone. Maybe it will be rescuing a kitten from a burning building or resisting the temptation of that one extra doughnut. Whatever it is, write it down!

Your Top Influencers

These are the people who influence you in a positive way. Think of the people who make you feel good and give you a smile that lasts even when they are not right there with you. I encourage that you keep this list updated and spend some time each day communicating with these people. Even if it is just an email message or a friendly phone call to let them know you were thinking of them, make the effort. This will feel good as it creates a positive moment in your day.

People to Thank

If you will spend just a moment to make a list of people to thank, it can grow pretty quickly. I want you to jot some down each day and make a special effort to thank them. You may be surprised how good you may make them feel, and how good that makes you feel, too.

Apologies Due

A proper apology can do a lot to help somebody else let go of frustration toward you. It can also feel like a weight lifted from you. Maybe you cut somebody off in traffic. It may be hard to give them an apology, but I want you to add them, too.

Promises Made

If you want to be able to count on people, you should first show them that they can count on you. If you said you would do something but think you may forget, write it down. Whether you said you would come to your son's ball game or you told somebody you would call them back, list it. At the end of the day, when you review this list, tally it up and if you missed something, add it to your list of apologies due tomorrow. We have each had a promise broken by somebody near us. It does not feel good to lose faith in others, and it is worth this effort to avoid doing this to somebody else.

Review and Reflection

Along with each of these basic lists, there is a scoring section. Be as honest and thorough as possible and score yourself each day. Beyond simply a numeric value, give some reflection to how you think and feel about your review. Are you maybe just a little better than you realized? Is there something you wish to improve? Give yourself a bit to reflect on these things. Simply the conscious effort you will make can create a great reward. Try it and find out for yourself!

Please note that if you already have the "Living in the Storm" companion book, "Diary of Betterment", you may use that more extensive version. The benefit to using this more abbreviated version is that it may be a little easier to create the positive habit. Either way you choose, it is still aimed at the same goal of creating joy and inspiration for yourself and others. One is simply more extensive than the other. "Diary of Betterment" also includes goal setting, efforts toward those goals, and a more comprehensive scoring and measurement format.

Always Wave at Fire Trucks

Try for a moment to recall the dreams you once had. For a lot of children, the dream of one day becoming a firefighter was strong. The thought of being a hero to others and saving the day is enough to last a while. Dreams go away and most of us get diverted by some other dream, or we allow our dreams to be stolen by those who love us too much to believe in us.

Maybe it was a firefighter, a police officer, a veterinarian, a teacher, or some other completely different dream that you wanted to achieve. In any case, wave your hand and smile when you see fire trucks. Let it be a reminder that dreams do come true, and that it is never too late to regain some of the youthful hope you once knew.

Your dreams will change throughout the storm of your life. Sometimes, the dreams will change into something even better than before. Maybe you are a parent now, and life is influenced by children. Maybe your career took a turn, and your schedule is hectic. So your dreams are different now, whatever the cause, but that is not to say that you must let go of hopes you had before. There are so many things that will shape your hopes and dreams, but none more important than the decision to create joy and inspiration in your life and the lives of others. Start it now, while your storm is still blowing, and begin to enjoy your life more than ever before.

I will give you one last story before I bid you farewell, until my next book. When I began this book, I did it during a category five hurricane in my life. I did so because I knew I would find more emotional attachment to the work, and because I knew I could see the storm clear enough to write it with purpose. I did it to show an example that even while the greatest challenges exist, you are never too short on time to help improve somebody's outlook … including your own.

If you will note the dedication page of this book, you can see that I dedicated the book to the life and works of Og Mandino. He wrote a book that was so powerful in my life that over fifteen years later, I named my first born son after a character in that book. It truly made me look at things differently, and at a time when my life was a real mess. That book is titled "The Greatest Miracle in the World", and it was given to me as a gift.

Although this message of "Living in the Storm" may not reach you on the level it is intended, I hope that it will give you or somebody you care about the inspiration to move forward with more confidence than before.

Days in the Storm

Life is a storm each day, from the time we wake up to the time we rest. Living in the storm means more than just being alive for another day, but rather enjoying our surroundings and making them better each step of the way.

The next pages will be your diary of progress toward a goal of more joy for yourself and for others. When you write it down, measure it, and follow up with actions, you cannot deny the efforts. This is intended to be the beginning of some very good habits that will help you appreciate yourself and others

I hope that you have enjoyed your read, and that you will continue with a better than ever life in the storm.

Day 1

Reasons for Pride

If you did something kind for somebody today, enter it here. If
you did something that reflects how you would wish for others to
perceive you, enter it here. There should be something to feel
proud about each day, so do not leave this blank.

1. _____ Score 10

2. _____ Score 10

3. _____ Score 10

Your Top Influencers

Enter names of people who influence you in a positive way.
Enter the score according to how many minutes you spent
communicating with them today, either in writing, by telephone,
or in person.

1. _____ Score ____

2. _____ Score ____

3. _____ Score ____

Promises Made

Did you promise to do something? Write it down before you
forget. If you break a promise, score it as -10 and add it to your
list of apologies due tomorrow.

1. _____ Score ____

2. _____ Score ____

3. _____ Score ____

People to Thank

Enter names of people to thank. This should be an easy list to make. We all have somebody to thank for the good things in our lives. Once the list is made, take action! Enter a score of -10 if you did not thank them, 5 if you thanked them verbally, or 10 if you thanked them in writing.

1. _____ Score ____

2. _____ Score ____

3. _____ Score ____

Apologies Due

Like giving thanks, it is common that we must apologize. If you owe an apology, write it here. If you did not give the apology, enter -10 and if you gave a sincere apology enter 10.

1. _____ Score ____

2. _____ Score ____

3. _____ Score ____

Review and Reflection

Add up your score and repeat this tomorrow. It should be easier to do again tomorrow. Watch your score over time and look for improvements.

Notes:

_____
_____
_____

Today's Score _____

Day 2

Reasons for Pride

If you did something kind for somebody today, enter it here. If you did something that reflects how you would wish for others to perceive you, enter it here. There should be something to feel proud about each day, so do not leave this blank.

1. _____ Score 10

2. _____ Score 10

3. _____ Score 10

Your Top Influencers

Enter names of people who influence you in a positive way. Enter the score according to how many minutes you spent communicating with them today, either in writing, by telephone, or in person.

1. _____ Score _____

2. _____ Score _____

3. _____ Score _____

Promises Made

Did you promise to do something? Write it down before you forget. If you break a promise, score it as -10 and add it to your list of apologies due tomorrow.

1. _____ Score _____

2. _____ Score _____

3. _____ Score _____

People to Thank

Enter names of people to thank. This should be an easy list to make. We all have somebody to thank for the good things in our lives. Once the list is made, take action! Enter a score of -10 if you did not thank them, 5 if you thanked them verbally, or 10 if you thanked them in writing.

1. _____ Score _____

2. _____ Score _____

3. _____ Score _____

Apologies Due

Like giving thanks, it is common that we must apologize. If you owe an apology, write it here. If you did not give the apology, enter -10 and if you gave a sincere apology enter 10.

1. _____ Score _____

2. _____ Score _____

3. _____ Score _____

Review and Reflection

Add up your score and repeat this tomorrow. It should be easier to do again tomorrow. Watch your score over time and look for improvements.

Notes:

_____

_____

_____

Today's Score _____

Day 3

Reasons for Pride

If you did something kind for somebody today, enter it here. If you did something that reflects how you would wish for others to perceive you, enter it here. There should be something to feel proud about each day, so do not leave this blank.

1. _____ Score 10

2. _____ Score 10

3. _____ Score 10

Your Top Influencers

Enter names of people who influence you in a positive way. Enter the score according to how many minutes you spent communicating with them today, either in writing, by telephone, or in person.

1. _____ Score ____

2. _____ Score ____

3. _____ Score ____

Promises Made

Did you promise to do something? Write it down before you forget. If you break a promise, score it as -10 and add it to your list of apologies due tomorrow.

1. _____ Score ____

2. _____ Score ____

3. _____ Score ____

People to Thank

Enter names of people to thank. This should be an easy list to make. We all have somebody to thank for the good things in our lives. Once the list is made, take action! Enter a score of -10 if you did not thank them, 5 if you thanked them verbally, or 10 if you thanked them in writing.

1. _____ Score _____

2. _____ Score _____

3. _____ Score _____

Apologies Due

Like giving thanks, it is common that we must apologize. If you owe an apology, write it here. If you did not give the apology, enter -10 and if you gave a sincere apology enter 10.

1. _____ Score _____

2. _____ Score _____

3. _____ Score _____

Review and Reflection

Add up your score and repeat this tomorrow. It should be easier to do again tomorrow. Watch your score over time and look for improvements.

Notes:

_____

_____

_____

Today's Score _____

Day 4

Reasons for Pride

If you did something kind for somebody today, enter it here. If you did something that reflects how you would wish for others to perceive you, enter it here. There should be something to feel proud about each day, so do not leave this blank.

1. _____ Score 10

2. _____ Score 10

3. _____ Score 10

Your Top Influencers

Enter names of people who influence you in a positive way. Enter the score according to how many minutes you spent communicating with them today, either in writing, by telephone, or in person.

1. _____ Score ____

2. _____ Score ____

3. _____ Score ____

Promises Made

Did you promise to do something? Write it down before you forget. If you break a promise, score it as -10 and add it to your list of apologies due tomorrow.

1. _____ Score ____

2. _____ Score ____

3. _____ Score ____

People to Thank

Enter names of people to thank. This should be an easy list to make. We all have somebody to thank for the good things in our lives. Once the list is made, take action! Enter a score of -10 if you did not thank them, 5 if you thanked them verbally, or 10 if you thanked them in writing.

1. _____ Score ____

2. _____ Score ____

3. _____ Score ____

Apologies Due

Like giving thanks, it is common that we must apologize. If you owe an apology, write it here. If you did not give the apology, enter -10 and if you gave a sincere apology enter 10.

1. _____ Score ____

2. _____ Score ____

3. _____ Score ____

Review and Reflection

Add up your score and repeat this tomorrow. It should be easier to do again tomorrow. Watch your score over time and look for improvements.

Notes:

_____

_____

_____

Today's Score _____

Day 5

Reasons for Pride

If you did something kind for somebody today, enter it here. If you did something that reflects how you would wish for others to perceive you, enter it here. There should be something to feel proud about each day, so do not leave this blank.

1. _____ Score 10

2. _____ Score 10

3. _____ Score 10

Your Top Influencers

Enter names of people who influence you in a positive way. Enter the score according to how many minutes you spent communicating with them today, either in writing, by telephone, or in person.

1. _____ Score _____

2. _____ Score _____

3. _____ Score _____

Promises Made

Did you promise to do something? Write it down before you forget. If you break a promise, score it as -10 and add it to your list of apologies due tomorrow.

1. _____ Score _____

2. _____ Score _____

3. _____ Score _____

People to Thank

Enter names of people to thank. This should be an easy list to make. We all have somebody to thank for the good things in our lives. Once the list is made, take action! Enter a score of -10 if you did not thank them, 5 if you thanked them verbally, or 10 if you thanked them in writing.

1. _____ Score ____

2. _____ Score ____

3. _____ Score ____

Apologies Due

Like giving thanks, it is common that we must apologize. If you owe an apology, write it here. If you did not give the apology, enter -10 and if you gave a sincere apology enter 10.

1. _____ Score ____

2. _____ Score ____

3. _____ Score ____

Review and Reflection

Add up your score and repeat this tomorrow. It should be easier to do again tomorrow. Watch your score over time and look for improvements.

Notes:

_____

_____

_____

Today's Score _____

Day 6

Reasons for Pride

If you did something kind for somebody today, enter it here. If you did something that reflects how you would wish for others to perceive you, enter it here. There should be something to feel proud about each day, so do not leave this blank.

1. _____ Score 10

2. _____ Score 10

3. _____ Score 10

Your Top Influencers

Enter names of people who influence you in a positive way. Enter the score according to how many minutes you spent communicating with them today, either in writing, by telephone, or in person.

1. _____ Score ____

2. _____ Score ____

3. _____ Score ____

Promises Made

Did you promise to do something? Write it down before you forget. If you break a promise, score it as -10 and add it to your list of apologies due tomorrow.

1. _____ Score ____

2. _____ Score ____

3. _____ Score ____

People to Thank

Enter names of people to thank. This should be an easy list to make. We all have somebody to thank for the good things in our lives. Once the list is made, take action! Enter a score of -10 if you did not thank them, 5 if you thanked them verbally, or 10 if you thanked them in writing.

1. _____ Score ____

2. _____ Score ____

3. _____ Score ____

Apologies Due

Like giving thanks, it is common that we must apologize. If you owe an apology, write it here. If you did not give the apology, enter -10 and if you gave a sincere apology enter 10.

1. _____ Score ____

2. _____ Score ____

3. _____ Score ____

Review and Reflection

Add up your score and repeat this tomorrow. It should be easier to do again tomorrow. Watch your score over time and look for improvements.

Notes:

_____

_____

_____

Today's Score _____

Day 7

Reasons for Pride

If you did something kind for somebody today, enter it here. If you did something that reflects how you would wish for others to perceive you, enter it here. There should be something to feel proud about each day, so do not leave this blank.

1. _____ Score 10

2. _____ Score 10

3. _____ Score 10

Your Top Influencers

Enter names of people who influence you in a positive way. Enter the score according to how many minutes you spent communicating with them today, either in writing, by telephone, or in person.

1. _____ Score _____

2. _____ Score _____

3. _____ Score _____

Promises Made

Did you promise to do something? Write it down before you forget. If you break a promise, score it as -10 and add it to your list of apologies due tomorrow.

1. _____ Score _____

2. _____ Score _____

3. _____ Score _____

People to Thank

Enter names of people to thank. This should be an easy list to make. We all have somebody to thank for the good things in our lives. Once the list is made, take action! Enter a score of -10 if you did not thank them, 5 if you thanked them verbally, or 10 if you thanked them in writing.

1. _____ Score ____

2. _____ Score ____

3. _____ Score ____

Apologies Due

Like giving thanks, it is common that we must apologize. If you owe an apology, write it here. If you did not give the apology, enter -10 and if you gave a sincere apology enter 10.

1. _____ Score ____

2. _____ Score ____

3. _____ Score ____

Review and Reflection

Add up your score and repeat this tomorrow. It should be easier to do again tomorrow. Watch your score over time and look for improvements.

Notes:

_____
_____
_____

Today's Score _____

Day 8

Reasons for Pride

If you did something kind for somebody today, enter it here. If you did something that reflects how you would wish for others to perceive you, enter it here. There should be something to feel proud about each day, so do not leave this blank.

1. _____ Score 10

2. _____ Score 10

3. _____ Score 10

Your Top Influencers

Enter names of people who influence you in a positive way. Enter the score according to how many minutes you spent communicating with them today, either in writing, by telephone, or in person.

1. _____ Score _____

2. _____ Score _____

3. _____ Score _____

Promises Made

Did you promise to do something? Write it down before you forget. If you break a promise, score it as -10 and add it to your list of apologies due tomorrow.

1. _____ Score _____

2. _____ Score _____

3. _____ Score _____

People to Thank

Enter names of people to thank. This should be an easy list to make. We all have somebody to thank for the good things in our lives. Once the list is made, take action! Enter a score of -10 if you did not thank them, 5 if you thanked them verbally, or 10 if you thanked them in writing.

1. _____ Score _____

2. _____ Score _____

3. _____ Score _____

Apologies Due

Like giving thanks, it is common that we must apologize. If you owe an apology, write it here. If you did not give the apology, enter -10 and if you gave a sincere apology enter 10.

1. _____ Score _____

2. _____ Score _____

3. _____ Score _____

Review and Reflection

Add up your score and repeat this tomorrow. It should be easier to do again tomorrow. Watch your score over time and look for improvements.

Notes:

_____

_____

_____

Today's Score _____

Day 9

Reasons for Pride

If you did something kind for somebody today, enter it here. If you did something that reflects how you would wish for others to perceive you, enter it here. There should be something to feel proud about each day, so do not leave this blank.

1. _____ Score 10

2. _____ Score 10

3. _____ Score 10

Your Top Influencers

Enter names of people who influence you in a positive way. Enter the score according to how many minutes you spent communicating with them today, either in writing, by telephone, or in person.

1. _____ Score _____

2. _____ Score _____

3. _____ Score _____

Promises Made

Did you promise to do something? Write it down before you forget. If you break a promise, score it as -10 and add it to your list of apologies due tomorrow.

1. _____ Score _____

2. _____ Score _____

3. _____ Score _____

People to Thank

Enter names of people to thank. This should be an easy list to make. We all have somebody to thank for the good things in our lives. Once the list is made, take action! Enter a score of -10 if you did not thank them, 5 if you thanked them verbally, or 10 if you thanked them in writing.

1. _____ Score ____

2. _____ Score ____

3. _____ Score ____

Apologies Due

Like giving thanks, it is common that we must apologize. If you owe an apology, write it here. If you did not give the apology, enter -10 and if you gave a sincere apology enter 10.

1. _____ Score ____

2. _____ Score ____

3. _____ Score ____

Review and Reflection

Add up your score and repeat this tomorrow. It should be easier to do again tomorrow. Watch your score over time and look for improvements.

Notes:

_____

_____

_____

Today's Score _____

Day 10

Reasons for Pride

If you did something kind for somebody today, enter it here. If you did something that reflects how you would wish for others to perceive you, enter it here. There should be something to feel proud about each day, so do not leave this blank.

1. _____ Score 10

2. _____ Score 10

3. _____ Score 10

Your Top Influencers

Enter names of people who influence you in a positive way. Enter the score according to how many minutes you spent communicating with them today, either in writing, by telephone, or in person.

1. _____ Score ____

2. _____ Score ____

3. _____ Score ____

Promises Made

Did you promise to do something? Write it down before you forget. If you break a promise, score it as -10 and add it to your list of apologies due tomorrow.

1. _____ Score ____

2. _____ Score ____

3. _____ Score ____

People to Thank

Enter names of people to thank. This should be an easy list to make. We all have somebody to thank for the good things in our lives. Once the list is made, take action! Enter a score of -10 if you did not thank them, 5 if you thanked them verbally, or 10 if you thanked them in writing.

1. _____ Score _____

2. _____ Score _____

3. _____ Score _____

Apologies Due

Like giving thanks, it is common that we must apologize. If you owe an apology, write it here. If you did not give the apology, enter -10 and if you gave a sincere apology enter 10.

1. _____ Score _____

2. _____ Score _____

3. _____ Score _____

Review and Reflection

Add up your score and repeat this tomorrow. It should be easier to do again tomorrow. Watch your score over time and look for improvements.

Notes:

_____

_____

_____

Today's Score _____

Day 11

Reasons for Pride

If you did something kind for somebody today, enter it here. If you did something that reflects how you would wish for others to perceive you, enter it here. There should be something to feel proud about each day, so do not leave this blank.

1. _____ Score 10

2. _____ Score 10

3. _____ Score 10

Your Top Influencers

Enter names of people who influence you in a positive way. Enter the score according to how many minutes you spent communicating with them today, either in writing, by telephone, or in person.

1. _____ Score _____

2. _____ Score _____

3. _____ Score _____

Promises Made

Did you promise to do something? Write it down before you forget. If you break a promise, score it as -10 and add it to your list of apologies due tomorrow.

1. _____ Score _____

2. _____ Score _____

3. _____ Score _____

People to Thank

Enter names of people to thank. This should be an easy list to make. We all have somebody to thank for the good things in our lives. Once the list is made, take action! Enter a score of -10 if you did not thank them, 5 if you thanked them verbally, or 10 if you thanked them in writing.

1. _____ Score _____

2. _____ Score _____

3. _____ Score _____

Apologies Due

Like giving thanks, it is common that we must apologize. If you owe an apology, write it here. If you did not give the apology, enter -10 and if you gave a sincere apology enter 10.

1. _____ Score _____

2. _____ Score _____

3. _____ Score _____

Review and Reflection

Add up your score and repeat this tomorrow. It should be easier to do again tomorrow. Watch your score over time and look for improvements.

Notes:

_____

_____

_____

Today's Score _____

Day 12

Reasons for Pride

If you did something kind for somebody today, enter it here. If you did something that reflects how you would wish for others to perceive you, enter it here. There should be something to feel proud about each day, so do not leave this blank.

1. _____ Score 10

2. _____ Score 10

3. _____ Score 10

Your Top Influencers

Enter names of people who influence you in a positive way. Enter the score according to how many minutes you spent communicating with them today, either in writing, by telephone, or in person.

1. _____ Score ____

2. _____ Score ____

3. _____ Score ____

Promises Made

Did you promise to do something? Write it down before you forget. If you break a promise, score it as -10 and add it to your list of apologies due tomorrow.

1. _____ Score ____

2. _____ Score ____

3. _____ Score ____

People to Thank

Enter names of people to thank. This should be an easy list to make. We all have somebody to thank for the good things in our lives. Once the list is made, take action! Enter a score of -10 if you did not thank them, 5 if you thanked them verbally, or 10 if you thanked them in writing.

1. _____ Score _____

2. _____ Score _____

3. _____ Score _____

Apologies Due

Like giving thanks, it is common that we must apologize. If you owe an apology, write it here. If you did not give the apology, enter -10 and if you gave a sincere apology enter 10.

1. _____ Score _____

2. _____ Score _____

3. _____ Score _____

Review and Reflection

Add up your score and repeat this tomorrow. It should be easier to do again tomorrow. Watch your score over time and look for improvements.

Notes:

_____

_____

_____

Today's Score _____

Day 13

Reasons for Pride

If you did something kind for somebody today, enter it here. If you did something that reflects how you would wish for others to perceive you, enter it here. There should be something to feel proud about each day, so do not leave this blank.

1. _____ Score 10

2. _____ Score 10

3. _____ Score 10

Your Top Influencers

Enter names of people who influence you in a positive way. Enter the score according to how many minutes you spent communicating with them today, either in writing, by telephone, or in person.

1. _____ Score _____

2. _____ Score _____

3. _____ Score _____

Promises Made

Did you promise to do something? Write it down before you forget. If you break a promise, score it as -10 and add it to your list of apologies due tomorrow.

1. _____ Score _____

2. _____ Score _____

3. _____ Score _____

People to Thank

Enter names of people to thank. This should be an easy list to make. We all have somebody to thank for the good things in our lives. Once the list is made, take action! Enter a score of -10 if you did not thank them, 5 if you thanked them verbally, or 10 if you thanked them in writing.

1. _____ Score _____

2. _____ Score _____

3. _____ Score _____

Apologies Due

Like giving thanks, it is common that we must apologize. If you owe an apology, write it here. If you did not give the apology, enter -10 and if you gave a sincere apology enter 10.

1. _____ Score _____

2. _____ Score _____

3. _____ Score _____

Review and Reflection

Add up your score and repeat this tomorrow. It should be easier to do again tomorrow. Watch your score over time and look for improvements.

Notes:

_____

_____

_____

Today's Score _____

Day 14

Reasons for Pride

If you did something kind for somebody today, enter it here. If you did something that reflects how you would wish for others to perceive you, enter it here. There should be something to feel proud about each day, so do not leave this blank.

1. _____ Score 10

2. _____ Score 10

3. _____ Score 10

Your Top Influencers

Enter names of people who influence you in a positive way. Enter the score according to how many minutes you spent communicating with them today, either in writing, by telephone, or in person.

1. _____ Score _____

2. _____ Score _____

3. _____ Score _____

Promises Made

Did you promise to do something? Write it down before you forget. If you break a promise, score it as -10 and add it to your list of apologies due tomorrow.

1. _____ Score _____

2. _____ Score _____

3. _____ Score _____

People to Thank

Enter names of people to thank. This should be an easy list to make. We all have somebody to thank for the good things in our lives. Once the list is made, take action! Enter a score of -10 if you did not thank them, 5 if you thanked them verbally, or 10 if you thanked them in writing.

1. _____ Score _____

2. _____ Score _____

3. _____ Score _____

Apologies Due

Like giving thanks, it is common that we must apologize. If you owe an apology, write it here. If you did not give the apology, enter -10 and if you gave a sincere apology enter 10.

1. _____ Score _____

2. _____ Score _____

3. _____ Score _____

Review and Reflection

Add up your score and repeat this tomorrow. It should be easier to do again tomorrow. Watch your score over time and look for improvements.

Notes:

_____

_____

_____

Today's Score _____

Fourteen Day Review

Now that you have read the book and have spent the past fourteen days logging reasons for pride, and paying closer attention to those around you, it is time to recap. Do you feel that you are more in touch with others? Do you feel better today than you did just two weeks ago? If so, make it a long lasting habit!

If you found this format of keeping score to be useful, you may really enjoy the extended version in my companion book "Diary of Betterment".

Notes:

_____

_____

_____

_____

_____

_____

_____

_____

_____

_____

_____

_____

_____

_____

_____

_____

_____

_____

_____

_____

_____